"*Surprised by God* is a refreshing surpri[se] [expe]rience of loving Christ and yet not likin[g] [those] as Christians. This wonderful book he[lped] within me. Thoughtful, provocative and [...] [...thoroughly] enjoyed and learned from it."

—ROBERT WHITE
FOUNDER OF LIFESPRING AND ARC INTERNATIONAL
AUTHOR OF *LIVING AN EXTRAORDINARY LIFE*

"What I love about *Surprised by God* is that I was surprised by how raw, authentic, real and poignant it was for my life. I began reading it to review it but it ended up reviewing me! Rich's book should be read by people seeking God, new in their Christian walk to seasoned veterans."

—BOB BOUWER
SR. PASTOR OF FAITH CHURCH (RCA)
7 SITES IN THE GREATER CHICAGOLAND AREA

"I don't know anyone who can cut through the fog and see my blind spots more quickly and accurately than Rich Blue. Does that sound threatening? It would except that with surprising vulnerability Rich freely shares his own journey, failures as well as triumphs, and you soon realize you are in the best of company as he runs alongside of you . . . cheering you on."

—DAVID G. GOODMAN
PRESIDENT ENTRUST

"Wow! *Surprised by God* makes life-changing principles available to all of us who hunger for more out of life and relationships. These insights and skills have the power to transform your life. I highly recommend it!"

—BRENDA SALTER MCNEILL
AUTHOR OF *THE HEART OF RACIAL JUSTICE* &
A CREDIBLE WITNESS

"*Surprised by God* is personal, engaging, enjoyable to read, and also profoundly insightful. Rich Blue uses stories from the Bible and from his practice as a Christian therapist to teach how our relationship with God can be authentic and dynamic. If God feels distant, this book will help you encounter God a surprising and genuine way."

—REVEREND BRIAN ROOTS
CHRIST UNITED METHODIST CHURCH

"In *Surprised by God* Rich Blue articulates the journey all of us are on to become genuinely human as followers of Jesus. The honesty and candidness of his story leaves one saying, "Yes...me too...been there...done that." Rich helps us take off the masks of pretense and self-protective armor of needing to be right and helps us to see that we are "enough" in every situation because Jesus is "enough" in every situation. Thanks for this gift."

—ERIC SWANSON
LEADERSHIP NETWORK
CO-AUTHOR OF *THE EXTERNALLY FOCUSED CHURCH*
AND *TO TRANSFORM A CITY*

"Rich Blue delivers readers to a spiritual world as personal as it is unique. He is an up-and-coming leader in the puzzling labyrinth of existence both for Christians and non-Christians who hunger for an understanding of their relationship with the universe. Those who are fortunate enough to discover his ingenious book will find a magical power to transform life."

—QIGUANG ZHAO, PROFESSOR CARLETON COLLEGE
AUTHOR OF *DO NOTHING AND DO EVERYTHING:*
AN ILLUSTRATED NEW TAOISM

"Not only do we have a longing to love and be loved by other people, we also long to love and be loved by God. In *Surprised by God*, Rich will help you explore and discover that raw, honest, authentic, life-giving relationship with God you deeply crave."

—DARYL MERRILL
LEAD PASTOR CHRISTIAN LIFE CHURCH
PRESIDENT CHRISTIAN LIFE COLLEGE

"In *Surprised by God*, author Rich Blue "walks the talk" of his faith—deeply, passionately, authentically. Through stories from his own life, his counseling practice with individuals and couples, and scripture Rich illuminates the path for all of us to become "relationship-based" people, alive with emotional connections with ourselves, others, and God. Although this book may speak most directly to Christians, it has a powerful message for people of all spiritual/ religious practices: That God desires authentic relationship with us—unfiltered and unashamed, without fear of guilt, sin, or punishment. From admitting fears and embracing doubts to finding purpose and, ultimately, grappling with our faith (a lifelong practice), *Surprised by God* opens the door to life lived most fully, in deep, alive, challenging, and loving relationship with our Creator."

—PATRICIA CRISAFULLI,
NEW YORK TIMES BESTSELLING AUTHOR OF *HOUSE OF DIMON*
FOUNDER, WWW.FAITHHOPEANDFICTION.COM

"Through his personal struggles and the inspiring stories of those he has counseled, Rich helps us *feel* his growing intimacy with God, drawing us into a deeper heartfelt personal relationship with our authentic selves, our fellow humans and the divine within us - the journey of coming home. "

—JIM MORNINGSTAR, PhD

"This is a book you cannot put down. It takes you on a spiritual journey which defines your relationship to God and others. The book takes you deep into Rich Blues' life. He informs you of his youth, his time in the ministry and his work at CLE (Christian Life Enrichment). I am Jewish and this book speaks to all as its premise is universal: seeking the truth in life about faith in God and the reality of our imperfect but ever growing selves. It is a must read."

—DAVID MARC DREW
PRESIDENT OF DREW HOLDINGS

"Rich Blue has made an indelible impression on the culture of our company. He has led our leaders on the journey towards knowing themselves both emotionally and spiritually. His love and wisdom have facilitated powerful growth and a hunger to know God on a deeper level."

—MARC MALNATI
MALNATI ORGANIZATION

"Read this book! Rich Blue is one the best men I know and on a true journey of integrity and pursuing a direct relationship with God for the betterment of mankind. This book invites you into a similar journey of your own. Bravo!"

—SCOTT G STEPHEN
PRESIDENT - GUARANTEED RATE ONLINE AT GUARANTEED RATE

"We all dream of a better life but often the personal paths we choose lead to disappointment. Rich Blue uncovers some precious realities that will help you soar in life."

—PASTOR FRED SINDORF
SENIOR PASTOR NORTH SHORE ASSEMBLY OF GOD CHURCH
FOUNDING MEMBER OF RICH BLUE'S PASTORS GROUP

"Rich Blue has remarkably woven stories from the Bible with his own personal journey along with the stories of many of his clients at his Christian therapy practice. With biblical text as the backdrop, Blue encourages others to find spiritual meaning in their lives. He illustrates this by showing that the struggles one has in relationships today are similar to the very struggles of the people in the Bible--no easy task--and that everyone can make the choice to be alive emotionally. As a Jewish American, I find this book to be universal in its message that we are all on a psychological and spiritual journey. Blue reminds us to "look at ourselves as we are: magnificent, beautiful, wonderful, and deserving of love and being loved."

—ELIZABETH SHULMAN, M.A., M.ED.
DIVERSITY EDUCATOR AND CONSULTANT

"No matter where you are on your spiritual journey, Rich Blue, has written a book that will speak to you. Straight-forward and from the heart – Rich, a deeply spiritual man who lives his faith vibrantly, shows us with deeply personal stories, that when our struggles seem more than we can bear, this is where God can do his best work."

—DR. NIKOL (MARGIOTTA) HOPKINS, DN, FAARFM

"Rich Blue has refreshingly modern insight into Christian faith. To hear him speak is inspiring. To read his writings is eye opening. I feel blessed to know him."

—ERIC MASI
TORQUE / PRESIDENT / EXECUTIVE CREATIVE DIRECTOR

"Rich Blue helped me at a time when I felt very challenged in my faith. I learned to value questions more than answers and found greater richness and authenticity along the way. Rich started me on a journey of embracing the unknown mysteries of life, where real faith is required."

—MICHELLE ALBAUGH, PhD
HUMAN DEVELOPMENT & SOCIAL POLICY PROGRAM,
SCHOOL OF EDUCATION & SOCIAL POLICY, NORTHWESTERN UNIVERSITY

"Rich Blue has been one of my most important interfaith friends and guides. His perspective of faith, which is a key topic in this book, has been our most intriguing topic of conversation and helped me define mine as a dynamic and ever engaging touchstone. I›ve enjoyed the nature of discovery and wonder that his perspectives bring which has helped me make practical our common human quest of God as citizens of Earth."

—MUNZOOR SHAIKH
PRESIDENT, BANGLADESH6G

"Rich has had a significant impact on my personal and professional life! As a Psychologist, Rich has helped transform how I counsel others. He taught me the value of being a truth-teller and how to confront my fears while helping others do the same. In my personal life, Rich showed me how fear--being unwilling to take risks, robs me of the joy and fulfillment that God intends for all of us to experience."

—GARY GREGG
CLINICAL PSYCHOLOGIST

SURPRISED BY GOD

Emma, Enjoy & lets discuss your ajourney of faith.

A JOURNEY of DIVINE DISCOVERY

RICH BLUE

HIGHERLIFE
PUBLISHING & MARKETING, INC.

www.ahigherlife.com

Surprised by God
ISBN: 978-0-9907578-4-9

Printed in the United States of America
19 18 17 16 15 5 4 3 2 1

HigherLife Publishing and Marketing
100 Alexandria Blvd. Suite. 9
Oviedo, FL 32765

CONTENTS

FOREWORD

WHAT COMES TO mind when we speak of having faith in Jesus? What does it really mean to have faith in God's Son in the everyday moments of life, such as when you are experiencing conflict with your spouse or your children?

Think of God as a loving parent. Don't loving parents watch over their children as they encounter life, learn and grow? Don't loving parents want their children to experiment, skin their knees and become increasingly adept at living? Wouldn't God want us to learn and grow with each other? But, what are we meant to learn? How are we meant to learn these lessons? Is it possible our life is an experimental laboratory preparing us to become whole and complete like Christ Himself? If we are being trained, isn't one of the lessons to strengthen our faith?

Paul Tillich taught about faith as a leap—a leap we make in every daily choice. *Surprised by God* is a story of learning about how, in the face of fear and uncertainty, our choices in life move us forward with each choice being a building block of what it means to live by faith.

What does this faith demand of us? What is really going on inside us? Are there different levels of faith? In *Surprised by God* you will discover some exciting perspectives on these questions, and also perhaps some long-sought-after answers.

This journey of faith, so intimately shared by Rich Blue, will introduce you to phases of spiritual awakening that will indeed surprise you, but which ultimately will bless your socks off.

This is no purely academic treatise—though there is rigorous theological and academic material interwoven. This is a real, rare, everyday journey into living our faith—honestly, authentically, vulnerably, moment by moment. It will inform your everyday experiences and choices from job choices to fights with your spouse, friends, or children. It provides grounded, real examples of what it means to live by faith in a loving God. Reading *Surprised by God* will add layer upon layer of practical understanding as you voyage with Rich through his adventure. It will inspire and inform your daily journey of deepening, strengthening faith.

People often speak of strong faith, but what do they mean? *Surprised by God* provides a personal example of a man of faith developing a much deeper, rich understanding of his own journey—extending and strengthening his faith. I have always been moved by the work of C.S. Lewis and his mentor, George MacDonald. Each of their writings and examples have provided inspiration that has contributed to the depth of my faith, but neither has given the structure and understanding of levels of faith that becomes evident through the pages of this book.

I feel compelled to offer you a warning, however: This book will be dangerous if you pride yourself on your theology and seek refuge from the realities of life in generalizations and biblical references that obscure the rough edges of our humanity—the point where we most need faith, and where our faith can truly grow. There is theology aplenty here, but it is a pragmatic theology of the Living Christ, not a contest to see how many parables or passages one can cite to avoid personal exposure.

Certainty and refuge in theology have little to do with actively lived faith practiced when we are terrified of losing our jobs or furious with a co-worker. Sure, we can pray, but how often are we praying to be relieved of the responsibility to lead our own lives? How often do we beseech God in prayer to be saved from something—or someone—when we are really avoiding personal, full responsibility—when we haven't exhausted our capacities?

This book addresses these raw moments when we need faith. I say all this to invite you to bring yourself fully to this reading, to be ready to abandon old ways of thinking and behaving that no longer work, and to have the courage to "not know." In turn you will discover, through Rich's journey, the true grace of a loving God, and a faith that allows us to become intimately familiar with ourselves as the marvelous creations of our truly unfathomable Creator.

Rich's stories and teaching have stimulated not only my own learning, but my service to others. I expect that you, too, will find his book to be thought-provoking as well as personally moving. In addition to running a thriving counseling practice and writing this book, Rich has a message that translates to all Christians as evidenced by his non-profit service in the developing world.

Whatever your perspective, expect this book to provide daily inspiration, challenge, and courage, as well as comfort and connectedness. It will help you in reclaiming all aspects of your humanity as gifts from a loving God. Prepare yourself to get to know a Creator who sees you as a beloved child—living joyously, growing, and learning to live increasingly in His presence.

—Dr. Bob Wright
CEO and Founder of the Wright Graduate University
and the Wright Foundation for the
Realization of Human Potential

ACKNOWLEDGMENTS

I AM SO GRATEFUL for the many life guides who have appeared just when I needed them. Each of them manifests the presence and love of God. I want to acknowledge the ministry of Young Life and the inestimable influence of Gloria and Frank Haas in introducing me to Jesus. Thanks to Don Wilcox and John Bruce and the ministry of Campus Crusade for Christ. These men were the early builders helping to shape me into a devoted Christ follower. I also recognize Phil and Jeannine James for their patience and investment in me during my early years in ministry.

I extend a special thanks to my spiritual teacher Bob Wright. I have done counseling, coaching, and life with Bob since 1989. Bob was the original source of inspiration for me writing *Surprised by God*. I am indebted to him and his wife Judith for their support, inspiration, and investment in me. Thanks also must go to the faculty and fellow students at Wright Graduate University. It is there that I learned to think critically, write clearly, and express myself freely.

Thanks to Journeys, a transformational leadership growth group that has walked with me through this pilgrimage of faith: Collin Canright, Jon Fieldman, Scott Stephen, and Tom Terry. Thanks to Rich Lyons and the men of the Wright Men's Guild who have helped me hold the vision for this book.

I am grateful to my friend Patricia Crisafulli who has been

a source of strength and inspiration. Thanks to my agent and publishing mentor, Mark Sweeney, who supported me valiantly in taking *Surprised by God* to the marketplace.

I offer a special thanks to the staff and clients of the Center for Christian Life Enrichment (CLE). I want to recognize my senior therapists: Nancy Rollins, Gabriela Cantu, and Andrew Mercer. The CLE community has partnered with me over the past 10 years to gestate this book. Many of their life experiences illustrate the message of this book. I have learned, grown, and transformed through my relationships with you.

Thanks to David Welday and the great team at HigherLife Publishing.

How do I begin to acknowledge my wife, Sue Blue? I would never have been able to persevere in this big, hairy, audacious goal if it wasn't for you. You have been a faithful wife, friend, critic, and editor. You have been a steady source of encouragement and inspiration. Thanks for believing in me and being with me in the ups and downs of this project. Thanks as well for the support of my grown adult children Lauren Schifferdecker and Phil Blue.

Finally, thanks to my dearest dog friend and writing companion, Missy. I miss you.

INTRODUCTION

I HAVE BEEN AN athlete all my life, from the time I was a boy who was big and strong for his age, through high school and college when I was a fearless competitor on the football or rugby field, to my adult years when I have continued to enjoy physical exercise and activity.

Being a natural athlete, I always had confidence in my strength, stamina, and speed, which I saw as all the proof I needed that I could take care of myself. Throughout my college years and afterwards, I took pride in the fact that I was rarely injured. I counted on my strength and endurance to feel powerful.

Then things began to change.

When my son, Philip, was in the eighth grade, he switched from playing soccer to football. Since football had been my sport, I decided that a good way for me to not become overly involved with him was to occupy myself elsewhere—with martial arts. After about four or five years of taekwondo, I noticed that I was beginning to get injured, with pulled muscles in my groin and legs. At first, I thought it was all the kicking involved, so I started doing some flexibility training. But the pain of the muscle pulls only intensified.

During this time I had begun seeing a chiropractor who was also acting as a weight-loss coach. When I finally told him about the pain I was having, he tried extensive adjustments to relieve it. While other problems that he found corrected quickly, the pain persisted. In October 2007, he sent me for an MRI. When the results came in, he informed me that I possibly had a more serious problem in my hip than we had imagined. At his urging, I went to see an orthopedist who conducted his own tests and determined that I had osteoarthritis that had degenerated. I was a candidate for hip replacement.

I understand this is one of the most common surgeries in America today. For me, however, the diagnosis was a shock. I had played sports all my life and had never been really injured. So how could this doctor tell me that I needed a hip replacement when I was only fifty years old? I felt as if my very sense of manhood was being taken away from me.

Instead of accepting the diagnosis, I resolved to fight the hip replacement. So for the next nine months, during which I saw the doctor several times, I did everything I could: massage, acupuncture, working out, losing fifty pounds, and taking higher doses of anti-inflammatory medications. All the while I prayed for a regeneration of the cartilage in the hip joint so that I would be spared the replacement surgery and recovery.

At the end of nine months the doctor took another series of x-rays. When the computer screen in his office displayed the images side by side, even my untrained eye could see that my hip had obviously degenerated further. Devastated, I knew I was in trouble physically and could no longer deny the facts: I needed hip replacement surgery. After receiving some coaching about the next steps, I began researching the best specialist and the best hospital for this procedure. The answers to both questions were about ten minutes from where I live.

On November 17, 2008, I went in for hip replacement

surgery. My wife, Sue, and my daughter, Lauren, were with me at the hospital. I was prepared mentally and physically. Mine was the first surgery on a Monday morning, which I knew was the best time to be operated on because the surgeons and the assisting staff would be well-rested. I felt so good I was even able to joke beforehand with the doctors and nurses.

The procedure went beautifully. I had set a goal for myself to walk that night, which I did. Even though I only made it out the door of my hospital room and back, it felt like a marathon. I was exhausted, but exhilarated.

Sue suggested that I ask the nurse for some pain medication. She advised me to get in front of the wave of discomfort that was surely ahead of me. I assured her I was fine—better than I ever anticipated. Sue tried to talk sense into me, but I wouldn't hear it. I was flying high with a sense of well-being and confidence once again in my physical ability. I was so certain of how well I was doing, I sent Sue and Lauren home to get some rest.

"I'll be fine," I assured them, and said good night.

What I didn't realize at the time, however, was that the effects of the anesthesia hadn't worn off completely. It was deadening the pain I should have been feeling. Once it did wear off, I was plunged into an abyss of agony. The reality of the surgery—in effect having my leg sawed off and then attached to an artificial hip—began to set in.

All night in my hospital room I wrestled with the worst pain I have ever experienced. The hospital administered medication to give me some relief, but the pain was still unbearable. Making matters worse, the medication made me hallucinate.

I experienced the sensation of falling asleep and then I would awaken, believing that I had been out for an hour or two. When I looked at the clock, however, only a few seconds had gone by. This happened again and again, all night long, believing I was asleep only to awaken confused three seconds later.

As I battled the pain, though, I was never alone. Throughout the night, I was sustained by the constant feeling that God was with me. I had not been abandoned. As I grappled for answers, including to the most terrifying question of all—who was I in this physically debilitated state?—God was on the other side of my struggle.

In my agony, my mind turned to the story of Jacob in Genesis 32, who wrestled all night with a man not knowing that it was really God. The line that resonated with me in the hospital room described how Jacob held on until his unknown adversary dislocated his hip: "When the man saw he could not overpower him, he touched the socket of Jacob's hip so that his hip was wrenched as he wrestled with the man" (Genesis 32:25).

A New Path

Perhaps, as I did, you have found yourself at a place in life where things have not gone the way you planned.

- You thought things would be better. You have strived for success and achieved it in some areas, yet when you are honest with yourself, you have to admit that you are deeply dissatisfied. When

alone with your thoughts you are asking yourself
these questions:

- How did I get to this place in my life?
- Why did this happen?
- How do I get on a better path?

You wish there was some kind of guide that would help you
feel better about the choices you are making, that could lead
you to a better and more fulfilling life.

If you are asking these questions, there is hope! I believe you
are right where you are supposed to be. Your disillusionment
is a gift pointing you back to the ABCs of life—dynamic relationships with ourselves, with others, and with God.

I believe each of us was designed for a meaningful life.
Surprised by God is intended to help you experience yours—a
guide for you in discovering your most authentic self.

You will read about the comfort and counsel I have experienced in my relationship with Christ. You will learn about the
foundational principles and practices that can make your life
and your relationships work. You will co-voyage with me and
many others who are on this incredible pilgrimage of faith we
call life.

You will learn from the stories of my life, the lives of my
clients, and the sacred stories in the Bible. You will learn how
to build your life on the bedrock of grace and truth. You will
awaken to the feelings of your heart, and learn how to find the
joy and satisfaction that come from living by faith in the God
of unconditional love.

You will learn how to find meaning in the pain and hardships of life. You will learn that it is your privilege and responsibility to create ultimate meaning and satisfaction in life. *Surprised by God* has been written as both a map and a guide to the truths and tools that have transformed my life and the lives of many who have journeyed with me.

Joining the Adventure

Although growth and development is hard work, the efforts are well rewarded. You will gain greater peace and purpose in your life. You will feel excitement as you become more like Christ in every aspect of your life, living with faith and hope, truth and courage. The more you are willing to tell the truth, take responsibility for your life, live with intention, reach out for support, and do the work, the more you will know that all things are possible.

There are no quick fixes nor magical solutions; there are only tried-and-true practices that will help you overcome obstacles and reach your goal. This is the invitation open to you. If you are willing, you will have the ride of your life. Yours will be a journey to a life more bountiful in experience—not emotional highs that are unsustainable, but a deep, abiding sense of being in genuine relationship with God and others.

You will feel what it's like to be fully yourself, saying what is true, expressing what you feel, and asking for what you want and need. You will know what it is to be loved unconditionally and to have a sense of safety and security amid trials, conflict, and danger. You will have the unimaginable joy of having the most satisfying and rewarding relationships possible.

God's promise is not that you will be free of stress, upset, worry, or pain, but that you will be fully engaged in your life and supported in all circumstances by His grace and love. That is the possibility and the vision that is now before you. It is up to you to say yes to the journey toward the destination of a more Christlike life, with greater connection and aliveness.

LIVING IN RELATIONSHIP

Although I had grown up attending church, and always believed in God, it was not until I was in my teens that I saw the possibility of having a personal relationship with Him. But, even then, it was a limited vision. I thought God was most interested in me knowing Scripture, obeying His teaching, and having the right answers.

> Your disillusionment is a gift pointing you back to the ABCs of life.

Over time, I have transformed from a Word-based Christian to a faith- and relationship-based follower of Christ. I have discovered that insight alone is not sufficient for sustaining our lives and our faith. We need our hearts—our emotions—in order to engage more fully in life. Like any relationship, it is emotions and ideas that connect us.

With Christ, I came to realize that deepening my relationship required emotional expression—not the pretty, sanctimonious kind but real, raw, personal expression and sensing. Genuine emotional experience is critical to our fullest relationship with God.

The power of the relationship is in the persistence on the journey and the discovery, not the knowing: trying, failing, striving, reaching, falling back, and trying again—what I call grappling with God.

As a boy who loved rough sports, especially wrestling, I experienced the visceral joy of physical battle, the toughness of an opponent and what it took to overcome him. During my journey of faith, I have come to see a relationship with God and Christ as an ongoing battle with myself in my relationship to God. It's a battle to be the real me and express the real me, all of me, in relationship with Him.

As I have grappled with that kind of authentic expression of, and honesty with, myself I have deepened my faith and my understanding of the divine. This journey has taken me far beyond what I thought was possible within my own life and has brought me a maturity and intimacy in my relationship with God, as I have grown more honest and intimate with the people I care about in my life.

It can do the same for you.

God yearns to experience the person in you who feels the freedom and grace to approach Him with what troubles you most, recognizing that He is not only the "Mighty God" but also the "Wonderful Counselor" and "Everlasting Father" (see Isaiah 9:6).

As I share my own journey of faith in the following pages, it is my desire to join you in expanding your understanding of who God is and how much He wants to engage with you in a real and authentic way.

Through the lessons and stories shared, it is my hope that

you will become a more vibrant partner with God. I will talk about where I have been and where I have come in my spiritual pilgrimage. I hope you will find comfort in yourself when you see how far I still have to go in my relationship with Christ. The joy is in the journey as you learn how to rely on God's grace and truth to transform you into your most Christlike self.

> Genuine emotional experience is critical to our fullest relationship with God.

Join me on this adventure of divine discovery—find the God in you and how His love, grace, and teachings will empower you to have the life you have always wanted.

Chapter 1

DIVINELY DESIGNED RELATIONSHIPS

The Lord God said, "It is not good for the man to be alone. I will make a helper suitable for him"
(GENESIS 2:18).

WHEN I WAS growing up, I often felt that there were two very different people inside of me. One was strong and tough, rough and rambunctious. A high-energy child, I loved being active outdoors and playing sports. More than one adult would have labeled me as wild. At the same time, there was this other part of me that was sympathetic and tenderhearted. I was a natural caretaker and defender of those who were vulnerable and hurting.

These two sides of me seemed opposites, especially as I got older. How could I play sports fearlessly if I was also inclined to be a caregiver? How could I protect myself behind a macho image if I let my tender heart show? This dichotomy was uncomfortable, and I found myself wrestling with who I really was and what it meant to be me. Sometimes my wrestling was of a more literal sort—such as the day I thought I broke my brother Charlie's ribs.

When I was five years old, Charlie, who was fourteen years my senior, left for active duty with the US Navy. The day he left was the saddest day of my life. So imagine my excitement when I was twelve and Charlie came home on leave. I couldn't contain my exuberance at seeing my brother, who in many ways had been a second father to me, always taking time to play with me when I was little. I idolized Charlie, who in my eyes was this macho military guy, and I couldn't wait to show him just how much I had grown.

He hadn't been home more than ten minutes when we started to roughhouse on the driveway. At one point, I picked him up and threw him on the ground. Charlie didn't get up right away. The pain in his side was excruciating; he was sure one of his ribs was broken. Instantly, I felt ashamed for hurting my brother. No matter that Charlie assured me it was an accident, that we were just playing—and he was fine—I felt responsible for his pain. As my tender, caregiver side came out, I not only wanted to make Charlie all better, but I also detested how physical I had been with him. In my mind, there just had to be something wrong with me.

The tension between being tough and tender has always been a troubling part of my being. I was never completely comfortable with either part alone. To be so caring and open toward others was just too vulnerable. To be a real warrior, capable of inflicting punishment on my opponent on the playing field, I believed I needed to deny my gentler side.

It took me twenty-five years and much personal growth

work to unlock another contributing factor to the puzzle that was me: the abuse I had suffered in childhood, the memories of which I had buried deeply within myself.

I didn't know then that in order to make peace with all of me—to understand and accept myself just as I am—I needed to experience unconditional love. I was longing to be seen and accepted for who I was without conditions, but long before I could open myself up to that type of experience with another person, I had to allow it to come from the source of my being: God.

When I was introduced to the possibility of having a personal relationship with God, in my teens, the idea intrigued me and quickly drew me in. The more I came to know about Jesus, the more I could see parts of myself in Him. Jesus, to me, was a hero and a Savior, the kind of guy who could really "take it," whether that was standing up to the bullies who wanted to hurt and even kill Him, or fasting forty days in the desert while facing seemingly unbearable temptations.

Yet while Jesus was unquestionably strong, physically and mentally, I also saw in Him a huge capacity for tenderness. He offered people safety, security, and rest. He welcomed the little children and forgave the sinners without punishment or shame. At last, I had found someone to whom I could relate, who was tough and tender at the same time. Through Jesus, I began to make sense to myself. I found in Him the hope of having all my hungers satisfied. As part of the family of God, I mattered and belonged. Here was the unconditional love that made me feel safe and accepted. In Christ, I found meaning and purpose, and what would transform me—not to magically make me over into something or someone else, but to become more of who I was.

Over time, however, I moved away from the alive, joyful, and infectious faith I'd had as a teenager. I was insatiable when it came to learning all I could about God and the Scriptures. The more I learned, the further I moved away from my emotions, which I didn't consider particularly trustworthy. I was convinced that all I needed was my intellect, to become a master of the Bible, to know it backward and forward, and to argue the fine points of theology and dogma. I thought I had it all figured out. Once again, I distanced myself from my tender heart, and I put on my armor for battle—this time, I fought the war intellectually, armed solely with my knowledge of the Bible.

By the time I was in my early thirties, the God I perceived was one who demanded my obedience, who I thought was most interested in me knowing and being able to defend the truth as it was written in Scripture. But as I came to discover, my understanding alone was not sufficient for sustaining my life and my faith. I also needed my heart.

Through a series of life events, I became a Christian counselor. The journey since has been one of mutuality in which I have helped others and myself to heal and grow. This process has spanned years of counseling, coaching, and personal growth work, which I continue to this day, all leading me to finally feel the love of God in my life and a hunger to reflect it to others to the best of my ability.

I have been blessed over the years with a number of mentors and role models who have helped me in unique ways in my walk of faith. Over the past twenty years, Dr. Bob Wright, my mentor and life coach has held for me the vision of becoming my most Christ-like self. Through years of leadership seminars as well as personal growth and development work, Bob introduced me to me. He rejected my attempts at an inauthentic sales job of my false self and was only satisfied when I was being my most genuine, powerful, and truthful self. Through Bob's help and investment in me I developed the courage to face unimaginable fears and feel profound hurts. He introduced me to the mystery of a mature, adult faith and intimacy with God.

Each of those mentoring relationships has both mirrored and deepened my relationship with God. Today, my mission is to live and proclaim that God is love and loves us all. In my life and in my relationships with others I want to reflect the truth I have come to understand and embrace: that God wants an authentic and dynamic relationship with each of us.

God does not want blind and unthinking adherence to dogma. He desires a connection that is alive, vital, and challenging. Just as through the incarnation Jesus engaged with others, so God wants to be hands-on with us. In a safe, vital, and real relationship with God, we are invited to bring all of ourselves—our faith and doubts, our joys and sorrows, our strengths and the places where we need healing. There is no need to hide or be ashamed.

RELATIONSHIPS: THE DIVINE DESIGN

Created in the image and likeness of God, we are born with certain traits that encode us for connection. Even our personalities are shaped by the experiences we have with others. From our nature to our nurture, we hunger and yearn for safe, nourishing, affectionate, comforting, supportive, mature, and intimate relationships.

Yet we spend so much of our time trying to hide from others. As much as we long to be seen and known, we constantly try to conceal ourselves behind masks and façades. The reason, I believe, is that we see ourselves as flawed and lacking, somehow totally unworthy of being loved. We try to conceal our real selves, afraid of being perceived as objectionable and unlovable. Sometimes, we project a superior air to keep everyone else at arm's length. We hold back from our spouses, families, friends, and even God out of fear and shame. Sadly, we are disconnected from ourselves.

It was in the late 1980s when I joined a leadership development group in downtown Chicago led by coach and leading thinker in human development and transformational leadership, Dr. Bob Wright. It had been suggested to me that I participate in Bob's groups in order to become more alive and potent. This was the first time I had sought support and training outside my Christian community. I was confident that Bob would help me to learn and grow; however, I was reluctant to trust Him because I knew he would challenge many of my traditional Christian dogmas and beliefs.

I came to this experience being very comfortable with groups. I had been participating in them all the way back to high school, and I had been leading groups for ten years while I was on staff with Campus Crusade for Christ, a ministry for students now known as Cru. Bob's group, however, was nothing like any of my prior experiences. First of all, it was not a traditional group in which people talked about their issues or recent experiences. It was a type of encounter group. Bob called it an "assignment group," meaning people were intently focused on learning, growing, and experiencing genuine openness and honesty with each other, all engaging fully in the here and now.

> God does not want blind and unthinking adherence to dogma. He desires a connection that is alive, vital, and challenging.

I found it totally chaotic, confusing, and unnerving.

Although I pretended to be engaged, I sat back and observed, silently judging everyone else. I couldn't connect with these people. I saw myself as superior to them because of what I thought of as my faith. The truth, though, was that I was terrified! With their emotional intensity and angry confrontations, the members of this group left me feeling extremely uncomfortable. What I couldn't see, however, was that the source of my un-ease was not them but myself. My dis-ease was, in fact, the result of my lack of mature and authentic faith.

As soon as a group session was over, I would tear out of there, sometimes literally running down the hall under the guise of having to catch my train. One night as I rushed to leave, Bob raced after me and confronted me. "I know your game," he yelled. "I know what you're doing. You come across as if you are so caring and kind, but you're mean and judgmental too. You're not what you make yourself out to be."

I was stunned. I knew Bob was a dedicated truth-teller; however, I did not expect him to see through my camouflage so quickly.

My first instinct was to defend myself. But on a much deeper level, I had the completely opposite reaction. For the first time, I was seen and known. Though Bob's challenge, exposing me as a fraud to myself, seemed harsh at one level, he gave me the most loving of gifts—the truth. Only by embracing that difficult truth could I ever hope to break through the shell I had built up over the years in hopes of becoming invulnerable to pain and hurt. Only then could I truly connect with others, to see them as they were and to allow them to see me.

DIVINE DISCONTENT

From the very beginning, it was God's intention that He would share in and enjoy an authentic and intimate relationship with His creation. No wonder the garden of Eden was paradise. Adam and Eve were naked and unashamed, open and accessible, with no barriers between each other or with God. They enjoyed pure intimacy.

In the New Testament, the narrative of Jesus reflects God's desire for intimacy to be restored with His people. Jesus is the good shepherd, diligently gathering together His lost sheep. John 10:14–16 records Jesus' words: "I am the good shepherd; I know my sheep and my sheep know me— just as the Father knows me and I know the Father—and I lay down my life for the sheep. I have other sheep that are not of this sheep pen. I must bring them also. They too will listen to my voice, and there shall be one flock and one shepherd."

The longing for this garden experience is hard-wired into us. We experience it now as discontent when we are not living a big life, loving others, and fulfilling Jesus' promise: "Truly, truly, I say to you, he who believes in Me, the works that I do, he will do also; and greater works than these he will do; because I go to the Father" (John 14:12 NASB95). Jesus' mission was to introduce the work of reconciling relationships, so that with His assistance we would carry it on to completion—that we would be one flock again. And, we would experience a divine discontent if we were out of relationship with God and with each other.

When Christians do not experience this divine discontent, it signals that they have lost their edge. Their relationship with God has become too comfortable, which in spiritual terms means stale and dead. They live by rote and habit, with no impetus to trust God and live by faith. Hebrews 11:6 says, "And without faith it is impossible to please God." To experience a life of faith is to have a dynamic relationship with God and with others—a relationship that is powerful, alive, and stretches you to become more of who you were meant to be.

God, Guilt, Sadness, and Anger

All too often, however, we limit ourselves and our relationship with God. We won't admit that we have questions or concerns. Instead we deny or ignore them because we don't want to appear faithless or doubting. We fear that God will disapprove and get mad at us if we tell the truth of how upset we are about our circumstances—and what we see as His apparent unwillingness to give us what we want. Our fear of being punished or cut off squelches us. So, we pretend our relationship with God is fine, and we hide behind a pious mask.

Perhaps we feel deep shame that we could possibly want something more when we already have Christ in our lives. Judging our hunger as wrong, we keep ourselves from exploring it further. Instead, we are left with a faith that feels dry and lifeless, providing no nourishment for our starving souls. When we assume God does not want to deal with our discontent and would be offended with our upset, we inevitably grow more and more distant from Him. Our unexpressed resentments rot away the foundation of our relationship with God.

Brian had been wild when he was younger. It wasn't until he was exposed to the gospel in college that he made a decision to place his faith in Christ. Since then he had grown spiritually. He and his wife, also a Christian, both worked to raise their kids in the faith. But slowly, over time, his faith in Christ began to fade. Outwardly he was a loving husband, a good father, and an upstanding leader in his community. To most people it would seem he had it all together—yet, there was something missing.

Shame and embarrassment kept him silent, his secrets hidden. After all, who would understand how a person with this much going for him could be so unhappy and dissatisfied? How could he dare voice his displeasure when there were so many people unemployed, unable to have children, or whose children were acting out or in trouble with the law, who did not have enough money to put food on the table? Who was he to complain when others had it so much worse?

How could he share his sadness, guilt, and despair when he

was a Christian? He had been taught to believe his sins were forgiven and a place had been reserved for him in heaven. Yet could anyone really be a Christian and struggle with the secrets and sins which continued to haunt him?

It's one thing to occasionally lie or misrepresent an expense on your taxes. Who, however, was going to accept Brian if they knew he had been having illicit relationships with escorts for years? Would he even have a marriage, let alone friends left? Brian's concept of God did not allow for an honest forum through which he could process and work through his guilt, shame, anger, and upset. Without knowing it, his God had become incredibly small.

> Our unexpressed resentments rot away the foundation of our relationship with God.

What Brian wanted—what we all yearn for—was nourishing, intimate relationships with others and a life full of meaning and passion. As with Brian, it is not enough for us simply to place our faith in Christ and then expect we will experience all we want and need. Receiving Christ initiates connection with God, but it is only the beginning. It is analogous to getting married; a momentous occasion to be sure, but one that does not automatically unleash the fulfillment that the relationship has to offer. It is the start of the race, not the finish.

Many people like Brian secretly struggle with feeling guilty because of wanting more in their lives, even though they have supposedly found the answer in Christ. They are confused and often keep their dissatisfaction to themselves. They come up with a magical explanation for their unhappiness, such as the belief they are being punished because of some secret sins they have committed. Others who play it straight also struggle with feeling guilt and confusion around their want for more.

There is much for us to learn from Adam and Eve, who had it all. Everything was fine, except there was one limitation—one thing they could not do and, no surprise to us, they did it anyway. Even though they were without sin and sharing perfect intimacy, Adam and Eve still chose to rebel and run from relationship with God.

We are no different. We repeatedly blow it even though we know better, and our poor choices interrupt our relationship with God. We banish ourselves from the garden of intimate relationship with God and others—trying desperately to find a shortcut back. Since Adam and Eve's fall from grace, life has been a process of attempting to get back into the garden—to return to harmony and perfect intimacy with God.

God made sure that re-entry was not going to be easy, setting an angel with a flaming sword to block access to Eden (Genesis 3:24). Literature is full of analogies of people trying to find the gold at the end of the rainbow, the quest for buried treasure, lost cities, the Holy Grail. All these outward journeys are symbolic of our inner hunger and passion for an intimate relationship with God in which we tell the truth without guilt or shame, and feel completely safe, valued, loved, and accepted.

To take up God's invitation to be in relationship with Him, we have to start with ourselves and our journey toward personal and emotional maturity. We were molded by God in our mothers' wombs, and our personalities were shaped by those who made up our family of origin. We need to understand the impact of this process of development.

WE HAVE SINNED . . .

As we consider our relationships with ourselves, with others, and with God, we must acknowledge the influence of our families of origin. For some this was a harsh existence in which value was placed on physical strength and engagement in athletic or outdoor activities, not on connection and feelings, which were suspect and even ridiculed.

For others, like JoAnne, who grew up in a church going family, the emphasis was on being good and following the rules. Outward appearance of peace and harmony equated to all being right with God. As a result, in JoAnne's family, no one was ever allowed to voice pain, disappointment, or anger—or question why certain things had happened. God was seen as the strict authoritarian and a stickler for the rules, which was reflected in how JoAnne was raised.

As she grew personally and spiritually, JoAnne longed to get real with God by admitting her pain and upset, even though that broke her family's rules. What propelled JoAnne forward to more authenticity was reaching the point where she began to examine her perceptions of God. She saw that these assumptions had been formed in childhood, and her beliefs became projections which she placed on Him. Her relationship was with the God of her making.

She began to see that our beliefs about God, other people, races, genders, indeed any outward differences, are learned from our experiences as children from our families and other people who influenced us. We swallowed most of these concepts whole, and they have been buried deeply in our unconscious.

As we look at our lives, we may feel sadness and remorse over things we've done or failed to do. We have sinned—in keeping with the classical Greek meaning of the word: "to miss the mark." Time and time again we've been off target in our actions, behaviors, and life choices. For those who grew up in a strict or authoritarian family with little or no tolerance for error, our shame can stunt our psychological and spiritual growth. We are too afraid to risk making mistakes in order to grow and mature because we do not feel able to deal with the shame. Until we can be honest with ourselves and others about who we are and what we do and think, we cannot possibly feel safe enough to risk learning, growing, and deepening our relationships.

THE PATH OF RELATIONSHIPS

Most of us approach relationships through the lens of our compartmentalized life. Our family is here. Our job is there. God, if He's not off the radar altogether, is on a shelf in a separate place. Even many people who profess to be devoted Christians don't understand the interconnectedness of it all. They don't see that enlivening their marriages, or being more present with themselves and genuine with family and friends, will draw them into a more mature relationship with God.

In my own life, I thought that having a connection with God was all I needed. Every other facet of my life—my wife, family, friends, colleagues—would for the most part take care of itself as long as I was right with God. All I needed was to keep my eye on God in the safety of my controlled and compartmentalized approach. Or so I thought.

It was my daily practice to spend two to three hours praying, reading, and studying the Scriptures. One morning Sue interrupted my Bible study time with a cheery, "Good morning!" and I lashed out at her. "Get behind me, Satan," I hissed. How could she intrude on my precious time alone with God?

What I couldn't see in that moment was that while I was trying to connect with God through prayer and Bible study, I was not aware or concerned that I was alienating Sue. I had no idea at the time that I was terrified of real intimacy, of truly sharing my life with my wife. Instead, it was easier for me to lose myself in Scripture reading or tune out through prayer than to engage in an everyday, ever-deepening relationship with her.

Now I see that my relationships are inseparable—whether with God or another person. In fact, I cannot hope to grow my intimacy with God unless I am also growing in my relationships with others. As 1 John 4:19–21 tells us, "We love because he first loved us. Whoever claims to love God yet hates a brother or sister is a liar. For whoever does not love their brother or sister, whom they have seen, cannot love God, whom they have not seen. And he has given us this command: Anyone who loves God must also love their brother or sister."

We cannot hoard that love. In order for it to multiply and grow, like the loaves and the fishes, it must be shared with others. As we begin our journey to a closer, more intimate connection with God, the path begins with our other relationships. In fact, it may be dissatisfaction with those other aspects of our life—job, marriage, family life, or a lack of direction and purpose—that leads us to look at the absence as well as the yearning for the presence of God in our lives.

The Old Testament is replete with examples of God in direct relationship with people—Moses, Abraham, Jacob, and the prophets, to mention a few. The New Testament is built around the person of Jesus, who came to manifest God as a human being to the world. Jesus is all about relationships— with His Father and with His disciples. He also uses Himself as a conduit for others to get to know the Father. As Jesus said, "Anyone who has seen me has seen the Father. How can you say, 'Show us the Father?' Don't you believe that I am in the Father, and that the Father is in me?" (John 14:9–10). Through those words, Jesus invited everyone to follow Him, joining Him in the journey of experiencing intimacy with God.

Through Jesus we see how to have nourishing and genuine relationships with others, which simultaneously lead us deeper into communion with God. Even His works—healing the sick and performing countless other miracles—were all in the name of relationship. As Jesus explained, "Even though you do not believe me, believe the works, that you may know and understand the Father is in me, and I in the Father" (John 10:38).

In Jesus, at every moment, we find our invitation to meet God. As Revelation 3:20 says, "Here I am! I stand at the door and knock. If anyone hears my voice and opens the door, I will come in and eat with that person, and they with me." By reaching out to Jesus—our Savior, brother, and friend—we begin a relationship that will heal the brokenness and illuminate the dark places in our hearts with grace. We come to know God and experience Him in our lives as we become more Christlike. This deep connection with God then motivates us to become more invested in our relationships with others.

Jesus underscored this interconnectedness when He condensed all of the commandments into two: to love God and to love our neighbor.

A Shotgun Approach

Jack first came to counseling because of the profound influence of a man for whom he worked. Fred had gone above and beyond his responsibilities as Jack's manager, to invest in and care about him. As a result, when Fred invited him to attend a retreat offered by my practice, the Center for Christian Life Enrichment (CLE), Jack didn't hesitate. He was hungry and open for more meaningful relationships with genuine people who told the truth and cared about others.

Jack was a rough-and-tumble, straight-talking man who spoke with frankness about his life and his relationship with his wife, which appeared to be anything but satisfying for either of them. When I asked him about God in his life, he looked at me as if I was crazy—even though he knew I was a Christian therapist. God was irrelevant, he told me, completely off his radar. He had grown up going to church, but that was meaningless in his life. He didn't want a relationship with Jesus, whatever that meant. He wanted to be happy, to have more friends, and to get his wife to change so they could have a more exciting relationship.

The good news for Jack, and the rest of us, is that because our relationships with each other and God are entwined, any improvement in one will benefit the other. As I have found repeatedly in my practice, as we become more honest, accountable, and authentic in our relationships with ourselves and others, we inevitably encounter God—although we may not label the experience as "God."

For Jack, entertaining the possibility of a relationship with God came through experiencing the tenderness and caring of others in the personal growth group he joined at CLE. To an outsider, this salt-of-the-earth outdoorsman might have seemed to be an unlikely candidate for group counseling in a Christian practice. But there he was at every session, often showing up early even though he had an hour or more drive to attend. He was always engaged and present. With his typical frankness, he spoke of his early life in which there was little caring or tenderness. A truth-teller by nature, Jack minced no words when it came to owning up to the vices of his life.

As others in the group overcame the shock of Jack's candor and forthrightness, they were powerfully drawn into relationship with him. For the first time in his life, Jack felt loved and accepted for who he was, and his heart began to soften. Over time he became more aware of his own feelings and grew in his sensitivity to others in the group. Jack developed the ability to speak the truth in love, blending his tough truth-telling with tenderness. Group members quickly recognized that Jack was Christlike in terms of his willingness to tell the truth—just as I had seen that same quality in my encounter with Bob Wright many years before. Over time others learned from Jack how to speak honestly and forthrightly, combining it with gentleness and mercy. As Jack grew, so did the members of the group; they modeled a sense of mutual love and concern for one another.

Members of the group often went to church and looked forward to sitting together. When Jack was invited to join them one Sunday, he reluctantly agreed. What moved him to attend was not a conscious hunger to know God. Instead, it was his longing for intimacy and closeness with the members of the group. Jack's newfound relationships with others led him to open up to the possibility of having his own relationship with God through Christ.

Moving into the light of truth no matter where we are in our personal and spiritual development, we are all journeying toward a fuller, more mature relationship with God. It is through this personal relationship with God that Jesus says in John 7:38, "rivers of living water will flow" from within us. He also was very clear that His purpose for introducing us to a relationship with Himself and His Father was that we "might have life, and might have it abundantly" (John 10:10 NASB77).

In order to experience that abundant life we need to move beyond the immature faith of our past, in which we developed our ideas of God based on our projections. This means pushing ourselves into new territory where we do not have everything all figured out, probing the deeper questions at our core of what it means to be loved by and in relationship with God. As we strive to become more like Christ, we will dramatically increase our capacity to love and serve others. Our life becomes an exciting adventure as we love, learn, and grow into the people God intended us to be.

To establish a relationship with God and each other, we need to move out of the shadows of our shame and into the light of truth. Otherwise, our need to stay hidden will stifle us. We will remain in a kind of emotional and spiritual kindergarten instead of growing in our faith.

Because Jack operated without much shame, he did not fear telling it like it was. This was one of the reasons he was so successful in his personal growth work. He said what he thought and was unusually receptive to taking in feedback. When he did not agree, he was willing to say so and lived with the tension of differing opinions. He learned to be honest in his self-evaluation and to see himself as he was in that moment. Because of his clarity and objectivity, Jack was able to move quickly to deeper levels of connection and greater responsibility in his relationships.

This sense of identity, security, and openness was a hallmark characteristic of Jesus. Repeatedly throughout His ministry, Jesus showed us the transforming power of admitting exactly where we are and what we've become.

CALLING THE SINNERS

If ever there was a guy whom people loved to hate in Jesus' time, it was Zacchaeus. The chief tax collector, he had made himself wealthy by overcharging and exploiting his fellow countrymen. Making it even worse, he was one of them—a

Jew, a member of their own community, but he had aligned himself with the Romans.

Then Jesus came to town, as we read in Luke 19:1–10. As Jesus passed through Jericho everyone was astir. His reputation as a wise rabbi and a healer had preceded Him. We can imagine the speculation and conjecture: Was this Jesus the one who had been promised? Could He be the Messiah who would restore the kingdom on earth?

Zacchaeus wasn't immune to the excitement around Jesus' arrival. He too wanted to see Jesus. But Zacchaeus was short and could not see above the crowd. He knew that in order to get even a glimpse of Jesus he had to get ahead of everyone. So off he went, running through the streets. He must have been quite a sight for those used to seeing him move about with his entourage.

As the crowd drew near, Zacchaeus realized he was going to get swallowed up by the throng and never accomplish his goal of seeing Jesus. He raced ahead and climbed a sycamore-fig tree. We can picture Zacchaeus, short and probably round, in his finest tunic and sandals, hoisting himself up into the branches. Here was the rich tax collector who hobnobbed with the Roman officials and lorded his power and influence over everyone else, hanging off the branches of a tree like a child.

In fact, in his hunger to see Jesus, Zacchaeus gave into the childlike yearnings that all the wealth and power and influence he enjoyed could not fulfill. Jesus responded to Zacchaeus' unexpressed hungers—his desire for belonging, acceptance, and significance—with fellowship and acceptance. In spite of Zacchaeus' sins, and exactly as he was—a foolish spectacle stuck up in a tree—Jesus offered him the gift of community and relationship.

When Jesus reached the spot, He looked up and said to him, "Zacchaeus, come down immediately. I must stay at your house today" (v. 5).

Zacchaeus scrambled down and welcomed Him gladly. There was no hesitation or second thought. He got down from the tree as quickly as he got up it.

Jesus' actions, however, shocked the crowd. Of all the people in Jericho, why would this holy man of God want to be the guest of someone so despised, who had turned his back on his own people? "All the people saw this and began to mutter, 'He has gone to be a guest of a sinner'" (v. 7).

The compassion and acceptance that Zacchaeus experienced from Jesus sparked a powerful conversion. Zacchaeus renounced his former ways on the spot, without being coerced. As Zacchaeus told Jesus, "Look, Lord! Here and now I give half of my possessions to the poor, and if I have cheated anybody out of anything, I will pay back four times the amount" (v. 8).Here and Now

What powerful words Zacchaeus uttered, proclaiming to all who would listen that he had had a change of heart, in the here and now of that moment—thereby signifying the authenticity of his newfound faith and love for Christ. With no apparent encouragement from Jesus, Zacchaeus was moved to address the suffering of the poor, as well as going above and beyond to make amends to those he had defrauded.

The story of Zacchaeus gladdens our hearts and restores our hope. No matter how far we've strayed, or what we've done or failed to do, Jesus reaches out to re-establish relationship with us. He knows us and remembers our name. We are God's, and we are forever welcome to come home.

Jesus is not just interested in relationships with those who see themselves as righteous and better than others. In fact, Jesus said, "It is not the healthy who need a doctor, but the sick. I have not come to call the righteous, but sinners" (Mark 2:17). Jesus was the great physician, more often healing broken relationships than broken bones.

KNOWING GOD PERSONALLY

Each of us finds our own way in our own time, as God works in us and others. For Jack, it came down to a beautiful summer day on the beach at Lake Michigan. Jack was there to support several members of his assignment group who had gathered along with Willow Creek Community Church to be baptized.

There were twenty to thirty CLE participants in attendance. As we listened to people giving their testimonies, watching them wade out into the lake to be baptized, I whispered to Jack, "What do you think about all this faith stuff? What are you feeling? What's keeping you from opening your heart to the love of Christ?"

On that beach he was standing on the bridge of the most significant relationship from his involvement with the group: his personal relationship with God through Christ. Having worked so hard on developing safer, more nourishing and mature connections within himself and with others, it was time to take the next step toward God by committing himself to Christ.

Suddenly, Jack took off his watch and handed it to a group member, and then he took his wallet out of his pocket. Shedding his jacket and kicking off his shoes, he headed toward the water with tears in his eyes. I followed him into the water where we met Steve Gillen, the pastor of the church, who embraced Jack and asked him questions affirming the commitment of faith he was making. With his usual candor, Jack answered them honestly, showing the goodness of his heart and the genuineness of his faith.

> No matter how far we've strayed, or what we've done or failed to do, Jesus reaches out to re-establish relationship with us.

Jack enthusiastically made his way into Lake Michigan, with members of his CLE group at his side, joyfully expressing his love for Christ. It was the perfect picture of multifaceted interconnectedness of relationships: Jack expressing his love for God as his Christian group-mates expressed their love for him, and he for them. How fitting that Jack was baptized surrounded by his community of fellow Christ-followers. You can't have one without the other.

It was a monumental occasion in Jack's personal and spiritual development, a culmination of many months of work and coaching. As significant as it was, however, it was only the beginning. For Jack, as for us, the work never ends in our journey to become more Christlike in our lives and relationships.

Although the kind of growth and development Jack experienced is hard work, the efforts are well rewarded. Applying yourself with similar honesty and commitment, you will gain greater peace and purpose in your life. You will feel excitement as you become more like Christ in every aspect of your life, living with faith and hope, truth and courage. The more you are willing to tell the truth, take responsibility for your life, live with intention, reach out for support, and do the work, the more you will know that all things are possible.

REFLECTIONS ON DIVINELY DESIGNED RELATIONSHIPS

- How would you describe your relationship with God: comfortable, growing, warm, distant, stagnant? Write a couple of paragraphs about it.

- What are the strengths of your relationship with God? Where do you want it to grow and mature? How would you rate your level of satisfaction and nourishment (1 low to 5 high)?

- Which parts of your personality do you have the most trouble accepting and why?

- Think of a time when one of your blind spots or character flaws was exposed or confronted. How did you respond: openly, defensively, trying to pass the buck? How did you take the feedback to heart?

- For what do you yearn in your relationship with God? And what do you yearn for in your relationships with others?

- Make a list of the strengths and weaknesses of your relationships: encouragement, insight, avoidance, judgementalism. Do you see any patterns and themes showing up consistently?

Chapter 2

GRACE

F OR I AM convinced that neither death nor life, neither angels nor demons, neither the present nor the future, nor any powers, neither height nor depth, nor anything else in all creation, will be able to separate us from the love of God that is in Christ Jesus our Lord (Romans 8:38–39).

Becoming part of Young Life, the Christian youth group I joined in high school, did not magically wash away all the hurt and pain I had inside, but it opened me up to looking at my life as more than just football, which had been the only real connection I had with others in high school.

As I immersed myself in Young Life—going to every meeting, participating in small groups, and attending Bible study—I got to know Mrs. Henderson. A mother of five and one of the group's leaders, she accepted me from the beginning as "one of the family," and over time became a spiritual mother to me.

Although I was aware that her daughter, Patsy, who was around my age, had a crush on me, I considered us to be just friends. After high school she and I attended different colleges, and she began a career as a semi-professional singer. While home from college one weekend, I was invited to attend one of Patsy's concerts. Afterwards, she invited me back to her house. I had the impression that there were going to be other people there. When I got to the house, however, Patsy and I were alone. Pretty soon things were getting hot and heavy between us.

Then Mrs. Henderson walked in.

The moment she looked at me, I felt like a dog that had jumped the fence. I was the guy who was allowed to be in the house at any time, and I had violated that trust.

"Get out of here, right now!" Mrs. Henderson yelled.

I tore out of there as fast as I could. I got in my car and drove back to school, all the while kicking myself for how stupid I had been. My whole life to that point had been spent avoiding circumstances that could get me into trouble. It wasn't that I was so virtuous; I just wanted to appear good and not get caught doing anything wrong so people wouldn't be mad at me.

After a sleepless night, I called Mrs. Henderson the next morning and told her I needed to talk with her.

"I would love to talk with you," she told me.

When I pulled into the driveway, Mrs. Henderson opened the front door to her house and greeted me. As I approached, my tears flowed. I couldn't say anything other than how sorry I was. Putting her arms around me, Mrs. Henderson assured me she understood what had happened. All was well, and our relationship was restored.

Here was an experience unlike anything that had ever

happened to me before. Here was forgiveness and acceptance in spite of the fact that I had violated the trust of someone whose opinion of me mattered very much. Here was love that was not dependent on being good or compliant. Here was grace.

THE PRODIGAL SON REVISITED

We are a people in need of grace. We may call it by different names: forgiveness, acceptance, compassion, mercy. To use a far simpler and more universal term, grace is an experience of agape love—completely unexpected and totally undeserved.

The challenge for many of us is that to really know grace we have to be "out there"—beyond the safe borders of conformity and the norms. In other words, we have to break the rules and experience our own brokenness in order to be made whole again through grace. Just like the fish that can only understand water when it's suddenly cast upon the shore, we can only know the enormity of God's grace when we find ourselves out of our element.

This thinking is not only paradoxical, it is downright scary. We are far more comfortable being compliant so that we don't make God or someone else mad at us. So we manipulate and appease and try to appear "good" by being obedient. These behaviors, however, are not grounded in love and grace. They are based in fear that one day people will find out just

> Grace is an experience of agape love—completely unexpected and totally undeserved.

how flawed we are. For many, if not most of us, it seems we are just one mistake away from being forever prevented from securing the love and acceptance we so desperately want, held just beyond our desperate reach.

Of all the stories of parental love, grace, and healing in the Scriptures, one of the best known is the parable of someone commonly called the "prodigal son." As the story goes in Luke 15:11–31, a man had two sons. One day his younger son asked for his share of the inheritance. This was quite an audacious move, because the cultural norm would be for the older son to inherit everything upon the father's death and then distribute a portion to the younger brother. Even though the father must have had his suspicions that his younger son wasn't going to make the best choices, he was willing to go along with what the young man thought he wanted. How else was his son going to discover what he truly needed?

After the father divided his property, the younger son went off and squandered the money on wild living while the older son stayed at home. The initial result was rather predictable: The good times only lasted as long as the money did. Then the younger son's so-called happiness disappeared and the proverbial party was over.

After he had spent everything, there was a severe famine in that whole country, and he began to be in need. So he went and hired himself out to a citizen of that country, who sent him to his fields to feed pigs. He longed to fill his stomach with the pods that the pigs were eating, but no one gave him anything.

The father, we imagine, had spent many weeks and months

expectantly praying and waiting for his son's return. All the while, he did not interfere with his younger son's free will. He showed respect for the boy's right to make his own decisions and learn from the consequences of his actions. He did not write off, condemn, or forget the young man. Nor did he try to find him and do whatever he could to rescue him. The father had faith that the time would come when his son would return home.

"When he [the younger son] came to his senses, he said, 'How many of my father's hired men have food to spare, and here I am starving to death! I will set out and go back to my father and say to him: Father, I have sinned against heaven and against you. I am no longer worthy to be called your son; make me like one of your hired servants.' So he got up and went to his father" (vv. 17–20).

The son realized his mistakes: he had messed up, lost it all, and hungered for home. He didn't expect to return as his father's son; he felt too undeserving for that. He knew his circumstances were the result of his own choices—he had no one to blame. Shame, the expectation of judgment and condemnation, kept him from even entertaining the possibility of being restored to his position as his father's son. His only hope was to somehow pay his father back and make things right through his servitude.

Looking down the road, the way he had every day, the father saw his son in the distance and was filled with compassion for him; he ran to his son, threw his arms around him and kissed him. Because the father understood his son's need to learn from his choices, he had not interfered. As soon as the son made the first move, however, the father was right there to respond with love and acceptance. He wasn't concerned about what the younger son had done; in fact, he even interrupted and prevented his confession. All he cared about is that the younger son had come home, and now he had the opportunity to rebuild and restore their relationship.

"The father said to his servants, 'Quick! Bring the best robe and put it on him. Put a ring on his finger and sandals on his feet. Bring the fattened calf and kill it. Let's have a feast and celebrate. For this son of mine was dead and is alive again; he was lost and is found.' So they began to celebrate" (vv. 22–24).

This, of course, is how God feels toward each of us. When we sin, when we make poor choices and take unreasonable risks, when we willfully do what we know is wrong, or are hurtful to ourselves and others, God does not seem to interfere and prevent us from making our own decisions. Nor does He get in the way of us experiencing the consequences of our actions. He waits for the right moment when we have learned our lesson and have made our move back to Him. When we are humble and ready to respond to his persistent knock and open the door even a crack, He rushes in.

The older brother, meanwhile, was not exactly thrilled that his brother was back home. As the older son saw it, he had been the good son who was nothing but compliant, doing everything his father asked. Now all the attention was on the younger son who was being rewarded—or so it seemed to him—for breaking all the rules. He couldn't believe that his father was not only taking the younger son back, but was actually throwing a party for him.

"The older brother became angry and refused to go in. So his father went out and pleaded with him. But he answered his father, 'Look! All these years I've been slaving for you and never disobeyed your orders. Yet you never gave me even a young goat so I could celebrate with my friends. But when this son of yours who has squandered your property with prostitutes comes home, you kill the fattened calf for him!'" (vv. 28–30).

Finally, the older brother had gotten honest. The hidden resentments that had been festering in his heart erupted, as a result of his worst nightmare happening right before his eyes. Until then, the older son had not been engaged in an honest, straightforward, and genuine relationship with his father— sharing in the ups and downs of working together as well as concern over the wayward younger brother.

Rather, he told the father, "I've been slaving for you. . . ." He felt victimized by his father instead of taking responsibility for making his own choices. His seemingly faithful actions and service were actually incongruent with the resentments, judgments, and anger he hid in his heart. Clearly, the older son wasn't interested in an honest relationship with his father. He just wanted to be compliant as a way of managing and manipulating his father's reactions. And perhaps the older son also resented the fact that, as the responsible firstborn, he hadn't walked on the wild side and taken any real risks in life or made any big mistakes. Afraid to rebel and risk falling short—and in need of grace—he was left with a life of bland conformity.

Yet the father's unconditional acceptance extended to the older son as well, who was in need of healing just as much as his younger brother. Without lecture, rebuke, or any hint of condemnation, the father pinpointed the heart of the matter with his older son. He acknowledged his son's anger and disappointment, and reassured him that his attempts to please him with obedience did not go unnoticed.

"'My son,' the father said, 'you are always with me, and everything I have is yours'" (v. 31). With those words, "my son," the father affirmed their relationship.

He didn't stop there. He was invested in the growth and maturity of both his sons. Thus, the father invited the older son into a deeper relationship, teaching him about gratitude and sharing in all that he possessed while celebrating the younger son's return. "We had to celebrate and be glad, because this brother of yours was dead and is alive again; he was lost and is found" (v. 32).

UNCONDITIONAL ACCEPTANCE AND LOVING EMBRACE

Too often when we reflect upon this well-known parable we focus only on the redemption of the younger son. This view is too limited and robs us of many lessons to be gleaned from this complex story. Traditionally, the way it has been understood is as a judgmental examination of the younger brother who lived the wild life.

A more accurate view is that we are both of the sons. Sometimes we are the conforming older son who tries to do everything that's expected, resenting it all the while. At other times, we are the rebellious younger son, wanting to do everything our own way without really thinking about the consequences.

Focusing on the broader meaning, we see in this beautiful parable the healing and growth of both brothers. This interpretation also draws attention to the central character of the story: the father who seeks to foster a deep and increasingly mature relationship with his sons. Because Jesus was the one telling this story, we have to reflect on the message He wanted to convey. Jesus was not only telling the story of the redemption of two brothers, He was also showing us the unconditional love of the father, who clearly represents the heavenly Father.

Instead of focusing on how much God hates sin, the message is how much He loves us and wants to be completely in relationship with us. God wants honesty and personal responsibility. Each of us needs to do all we can to be honest and upfront with the Father. God can handle our urges, mistakes, judgments, and reactivity. What He can't handle is our unwillingness to be honest and our attempts to mask our true selves.

Often in our tendency for recrimination we cling to the story of the younger son, hoping to find proof and assurance of God's forgiveness of sins. If we can see only the younger son's need of the father's forgiving embrace, however, we miss the lesson of the older son entirely. We fail to see the times when in our self-righteousness we have condemned others whom we see as bad—or, at least, worse than we are—and when we have mistaken a show of outward conformity for an authentic and meaningful relationship. This is counterfeit Christianity.

If we dismiss both brothers as wrong, we also miss some very important lessons. The brothers are examples of two extremes: breaking all the rules and complete conformity. Neither is a healthy or mature way to live. Rather, we need a balance between the two. We need at times to take risks and to be willing to make mistakes in the process of learning and living our lives, and we also need to exercise caution and walk the straight and narrow path—knowing that at all times we have God's safety net of grace to keep us safe.

No matter how many times we read a story such as the prodigal son, the father's unconditional acceptance and loving embrace only penetrates the surface of our fears and limiting beliefs. Maybe for other people, we tell ourselves, but not us: "If I revealed my true nature—what I really think, feel, and believe—then God would not like me and possibly reject me. And then where would I be?"

The truth, however, is that God knows all about us, no matter how well we think we've kept our dark side hidden, and no amount of "good deeds" will win us any points with Him. Although God desires that we follow His principles and obey His commands, His love for us is a completely separate issue irrespective of our conduct. It is the result of His choice to be true to His nature and not the result of our deserving it by our good behavior.

Yet foundational to any relationship—with God or another person—is trust. To be in a genuine, authentic relationship we have to trust that the other person will accept us as we are and forgive us when we fail, which we inevitably will. Before we can really risk being authentic with others, we must embrace and digest the marvelous truth that we are completely and unconditionally loved.

It is a choice for us to make, and it requires faith. I tell people all the time that I cannot "prove" that God loves them or me. It is a decision I make by faith. There is evidence to support either position: that God is loving or He is not. Our choice is what we are going to focus on, and on which body of evidence we are going to base our faith. Only when we feel secure in His love can we choose to love ourselves and risk being ourselves.

From a spiritual sense, we do not have the capacity to trust that leap without grace. It is what allows us to look at ourselves and our relationships in the light of truth. With grace we are emboldened to take the first step to being real, which is to understand how valuable it is to be true to ourselves.

Opening the Door to God's Grace

When Al first came to see me he was struggling. Even though he was successful at work and consistently moved up through the ranks into management, he was unhappy and lacked deeper satisfaction. Something was missing, but he couldn't identify what.

Al was repeatedly challenged by the men he reported to who were part of a leadership/management development program. He sensed they cared about him above and beyond the job, and each of them had lives of meaning and purpose. They were genuine and straightforward with him. They confronted him honestly while being vulnerable enough to admit their own failings and struggles. These men encouraged Al to move into management and become part of the group training program. There he met a number of people who were involved in my practice. They were excellent leaders and also had a quiet, yet profound faith in God. Recognizing the hunger for more growing within himself, Al wanted what they were experiencing.

> Although God desires that we follow His principles and obey His commands, His love for us is a completely separate issue irrespective of our conduct.

In that moment, Al opened the door to God's grace. He took a first step out of the secret shame and pain of his past, which included his youthful involvement in a violent street gang. As Al became more truthful with himself and others, a sense of peace and calm came over him. Feeling safe was a foreign experience, even though as an adult Al lived with his wife and children in a nice house in a good neighborhood and worked in a company where he was valued and respected. Inside, Al was always on the alert and often on the run, just as he had been years earlier. To him, life was dangerous, and if he didn't look out for himself he'd have to pay the price.

Over time, and with much building of trust, Al began to share with others the story of his young life. Growing up without a strong family structure, he had been on his own from a young age. His faith tradition had left him with a lot of confusion and resentment toward God and religion in general. Without a strong faith center, and with only tenuous ties to his family, Al sought a different kind of identity: He joined a gang. At first he felt like he belonged and what he did mattered. He made it his ambition to move up into leadership—much the same way that, years later, he would be determined to advance in his career.

Belonging in the gang, however, came at a high price. Increasingly, Al began doing things that made him more and more uncomfortable. He was standing out as a leader because of his fearless dedication to serving the gang. The younger kids looked up to him. He was encouraging them to fight, sell drugs, vandalize, and steal. He witnessed boys he loved get killed, and spoke reluctantly of times when he nearly lost his own life. Over time he became increasingly conflicted about the life he was living and the influence he was having on younger gang members.

Al became more and more afraid, knowing that life in the gang ultimately offered him either prison or death. Fortunately, Al followed his inner voice, which told him the gang would be his undoing. He did what he had to do to leave the gang: enduring a beating—known as undergoing a "violation"—that could have killed him.

Admitting his past and his pain was excruciating for Al. In counseling sessions he began to share honestly the pain he was carrying and expressed profound regret over the things he had done and for influencing so many younger boys to follow life in the gang.

The exploration of his past ushered in a powerful healing process as he let down the walls that for years had shut others out while keeping him imprisoned. As he grappled with the things he had done, Al learned how to forgive, accept, and love himself. Al also discovered a greater capacity to feel, love, work, play, and engage with others. Grace helped him expand the possibilities for his life. In time, and with much dedication and hard work, Al moved beyond what had been comfortable and began to take new types of risks by becoming more honest about what he was thinking, feeling, and doing.

The healing Al experienced brought with it the possibility of having a relationship with God. He gained the sense that a one-on-one connection to Christ was not just a concept, but a reality he could pursue. By opening himself up to God's grace, Al discovered hope and a sense of belonging. As his relationship with God improved, he discovered more aspects of himself, and access to a much greater range of emotions—which significantly improved his family life. He recognized that the process was not finished and he was not "done." Rather, he continued to grow in his faith and his development, trusting that the grace that had carried him this far would sustain him throughout the journey.

LOVING AND ACCEPTING OURSELVES

No matter what we've done or failed to do, grace is the source of our determination to love and accept ourselves. We find comfort in God's grace and mercy, believing that through Jesus we find forgiveness that God so gladly offers. We hold fast to the words of Isaiah 1:18 that "though your sins are like scarlet, they shall be as white as snow; though they are red as crimson, they shall be like wool."

Loving and accepting ourselves is a dynamic process that begins with a decision—a determination once and for all to choose to love and accept ourselves. This declaration unleashes a moment-by-moment reaffirmation of our love for ourselves. It is a choice to be on our own side and to internalize Christ.

We learn to love ourselves without sentimentality. We speak the truth, but with a sense of acceptance of ourselves and others. We cling to the grace of God and the compassion of Jesus who ate and drank with outcasts and lowlifes, telling those who mocked Him for the unsavory company He kept, "It is not the healthy who need a doctor, but the sick. I have not come to call the righteous, but sinners" (Mark 2:17). For those who harbor secrets from their past, Jesus' words are a balm for the wounded and shame-ridden soul.

From her strict religious upbringing by an authoritarian mother, Monica knew right from wrong. As a book-smart but naïve teenager, she secretly prided herself on how "perfect" she was, that unlike so many others she did nothing wrong. What Monica couldn't admit to anyone was the deep pain inside: Growing up in a polarized household, with two parents who fought continuously over her father's infidelity, she feared she would never be loved. In a bitterly sad moment, her mother had once pronounced to her, "You will never get married. You'll be the career girl of the family."

Monica took those words to heart, turning them into a kind of emotional death sentence that determined she would never be loved. And so, years later as a young woman living alone in New York City, she settled for whatever crumbs of love came her way. Believing herself to be in love for the first time in her life, Monica began an intimate relationship with her boyfriend, Jean-Paul, even though she knew he was going back to France in six months. Soon after she and Jean-Paul began to date, Monica's mother was diagnosed with terminal cancer.

A few months later, Monica learned she was pregnant.

Fearing the judgment of her family, especially with her mother so close to death, and knowing that Jean-Paul was returning to his country and his longtime girlfriend, Monica decided to have an abortion.

The decision terrified her, knowing that her actions to terminate a life were displeasing to God. Even in the doctor's office, Monica agonized over her choice. Yet she did not leave the examination room where she waited alone, saying what she thought would be one last prayer to God, whose presence had always been palpable in her life. That prayer was interrupted when the doctor and nurse entered the room.

When they left after the procedure and Monica was told to get dressed, she waited to feel the abyss inside—the complete abandonment by God who now surely hated her. What Monica discovered instead was the same sense of presence that, from the time she was a little girl, had always let her know God was in her life. Although her struggle would be painful, particularly when her mother died a few weeks later, Monica entered counseling and began to explore what it might mean to seek forgiveness and to love and accept herself. The journey was long and hard, and she failed many times along the way, but in time she gained a sense of peace and forgiveness. Over the years, the healing of God's grace has allowed her to grow from an infantile level of "will you forgive me even if I'm bad?" to a deeper longing to imitate Christ in her life.

Like Al and Monica, we, too, have dark and painful places inside where we have failed ourselves, others, and God. As much as we try to hide and rationalize, something keeps getting our attention, drawing us back to the wound that we would rather conceal. That persistent, nagging, and hopeful reminder is grace: encouraging and emboldening us to get honest and admit our failings, knowing in the words of the apostles that "it is through the grace of our Lord Jesus that we are saved" (Acts 15:11).

We cannot earn God's forgiveness. We do not merit His love and mercy in any way. His healing grace, like His perfect love for us, is freely given because it would be utterly against God's nature as the divine parent to not love His children. Loving us, however, does not preclude God's sadness and anger at the poor decisions we make or the hurtful and hateful ways we treat each other. No matter what we've done or how far we've strayed, God always waits for us to return home to Him.

GRACE IS OUR SAFETY NET

Though we all long for perfect love and intimacy, none of us have ever experienced it, apart perhaps from some special encounters with God. Our parents were far from perfect in the expression of their love, and we in turn have fallen short of the goal of loving our children as God loves us.

Although we have rarely, if ever, tasted unconditional love, we still seek it. I remember early in my development as a Christian, my spiritual mother to me, said, "God will never love you more than He does in this moment." At the time, this concept blew my mind—and yet I took amazing comfort from it. God's love is because of who He is and not based on who we are or what we become.

Although we cannot experience grace "on demand," as if it came from some celestial dispenser, we know that it permeates our lives even when we are not aware of it. Therefore, we must rely on the knowledge of grace—the fact that we are loved by God, right here and right now, just as we are—to carry us forward. Acknowledging and accepting grace as a force that is— like gravity, or the supply of oxygen in the atmosphere—we can make empowered decisions to transform our lives in Christ.

The knowledge of grace gives us courage, and those occasional bursts when grace is tangible make us bold. We can reach out and claim the inheritance that is ours, which is nothing less than the Father's kingdom. Experiencing even a taste of what it feels like to be loved perfectly by the Creator who made us, we learn to love and cherish ourselves and each other. In this acceptance we find the encouragement to look more deeply within, to those hidden places of shame and regret, to move beyond the past into more aliveness and abundance in the future.

Without grace, we can do nothing other than wallow in our own self-pity and fears over what we've done or failed to do. With grace, however, we can begin to realize the promise that "nothing will be impossible with God" (Luke 1:37 NASB).

In all our relationships, grace provides a kind of safety net that allows us to stretch beyond our old limits. We become like the high flyers on the trapeze, who when learning new moves know that the net will catch them when they slip up and fall— and fall they will! Similarly, as we learn the skills and develop the character and faith to risk becoming truly open and honest with others—increasingly ourselves, naked and unashamed, and in relationship with those who have the capacity to frustrate, disappoint, and hurt us—grace is our safety net.

The path to intimacy with God requires us to learn how to be truthful, open, and alive with each other and ourselves. None of us can provide unconditional love for each other; however, we can have the intent to live up to that ideal. When we fall short and punish those closest to us by withholding, abandoning, and attacking, grace gives us a place to regroup, forgive ourselves, and redouble our efforts to become more and more like Christ. We reach out for support to learn the skills we need to get clear and current with ourselves and those we are in relationship with, making amends where necessary.

The grace you deeply desire and deserve is available to you in this moment—and in the next, and in the next. All that is required is your intention. Like the young prodigal son, it is enough just to turn our feet toward home. The decision is sufficient to start us on the journey toward our desired destination of greater connection to God. Yes, the road may twist and turn, and we will have emotional pitfalls along the way, but we will reach our destination because God greatly shortens the distance by moving toward us.

> We must rely on the knowledge of grace—the fact that we are loved by God, right here and right now, just as we are—to carry us forward.

This journey is not possible without grace. Our challenge is to live as if we believe it is true. The game of life is that you and I will risk making mistakes as we learn and grow knowing God promises, "I will never leave you nor forsake you" (see Hebrews 13:5).

REFLECTIONS ON GRACE

- Name the people who have been most influential in your spiritual journey. In what ways has each of them contributed to your growth and development?

- Reflect on the story of the prodigal son (Luke 15:11–31). Where do you see yourself in the younger brother who left home? In what ways do you identify with the older brother who stayed home?

- Describe an occasion on which you experienced transcendent grace—one of those "God moments" when there is no other explanation other than God was intervening in your life.

- In what area of your life do you most need to embrace and accept grace: in a troubled relationship, facing a particular weakness, or battling shame? Where would you most like to experience the freedom and forgiveness freely available in Christ?

Chapter 3

TRUTH

Then you will know the truth, and the truth will set you free
(JOHN 8:32).

I LEARNED ONE OF my most powerful lessons on truth by cleaning the bathroom. That was not exactly what I had in mind when reading John's gospel, but the freedom I experienced as a result of the lesson showed me exactly what it means to know the truth and experience freedom as a result.

The opportunity to understand my limited thinking about truth arose during a weekend retreat built around the principle of living in integrity. As part of the experience we worked in teams and maintained the living space. After we completed the assignments we met and reflected on how the lessons we were learning played out in the tasks of daily living and relationships. The focus of the work experiences was to confront and challenge a basic belief most of us share: that we are honest and truthful.

In "real life" I am known as an efficient, hard-charging, get-the-job-done person. I am thought of as having an impec-

SURPRISED BY GOD

cable work ethic. So it was natural for me to agree to do more than anyone else and to lead the housework effort in any way I could.

When we had completed our tasks, I waited with my team, packed into a small room, to discuss and learn from our assignment. Several facilitators who had been monitoring our work as a team were present. Their job was to challenge us to examine the extent to which we operated in good faith, living true to our commitments, principles, and values.

I was surprised at how scared I was. Given my strong work ethic, I had expected that I would be excitedly awaiting praise and recognition. On the contrary, I felt like I was back in the principal's office, terrified that I was going to get in trouble.

Time passed, and when I didn't get indicted I began to feel a bit calmer. I let down my guard. Then one of the facilitators asked who on our team was responsible for cleaning the bathrooms. Not me. I was not part of that group. The facilitator brought to our attention that the waste baskets in the bathroom had not been emptied, and when I heard "waste baskets" I felt it in my gut. I suddenly remembered I had agreed to make a final check of the trash in the bathrooms, and I had forgotten to do it. I could not believe that I had forgotten to complete my task.

It was my fault. I was the culprit!

I was surprised at the intensity of my fear. I felt like I was fighting for my life. I had blown it and left myself open to trouble.

What could I say? How could I get out of this mess? Certainly it would make a difference that I had done so much more than

48

everyone else on my team. I had worked the hardest and had done the most—that had to count for something.

I needed to stress that I had intended to empty the waste baskets but I had just forgotten. My defense was based on the distinction between forgetting and lying. I was working diligently and had simply forgotten one thing; it was that simple. I was not lying about my responsibility, and I was not going to let them intimidate me. I was determined to not back down.

During what became a sometimes loud fight, I found myself transported back to a time when I was young and being punished for something I had done. Now I was having all the same fears I had experienced when I was a child. I had mistakenly associated error with sin, learning to believe that there was something very wrong with me if I made any kind of error. I had made it my aim to avoid making mistakes at all costs.

Gradually, the persistence of the facilitators and my teammates broke through my resistance. I realized that they were investing in me and not trying to humiliate me. I had a choice: to admit that I had failed and accept myself in the process, or scramble to defend and deny my responsibility. When I finally broke down—broke free—it became the gateway to an unexpected experience of grace and forgiveness.

I saw the personal cost of my motivation to perform out of a desire to avoid getting punished. My inability to love and accept myself prevented me from admitting that I had made a mistake, which in turn robbed me of the joy of discovering that the world was both a classroom and a playground in which I could try new things, make mistakes, learn, and grow.

I learned that I—not God or other people—am my harshest critic.

Truth Reveals Us as Flawed

Truth and grace provide the foundation for all relationships. Without grace, we cannot look at ourselves honestly, as we really are, and express our truth. Without truth, we cannot be authentic and genuine, open and vulnerable. Without these capabilities, we cannot be in relationship with God, with others, or even with ourselves. If we are honest—truth-telling— we would admit that we are afraid of the truth. We fear that we—and others—cannot handle our truth. If people really knew what we said, did, or thought, they could never accept or love us. We would be rejected and despised by everyone, especially God. Therefore we hide—not with overt lies, but with partial truths and excuses that we think are more acceptable to others. Most people, including myself, view lying as wrong. We may acknowledge that, on occasion, we bend the truth or omit something here or there, but we consider that's normal, far from being a liar. But the truth is, we are all liars!

Truth is what is—fully and deeply. Jesus is the way, the truth, and the life. In comparison, the truth reveals us as flawed individuals who are in need of grace and healing, and it expresses the enormity of God's unconditional love for us. Truth is a goal toward which we orient ourselves as we are emboldened to see, say, and be more than we ever thought possible. Truth becomes our highest vision for ourselves and the world.

Accordingly, truth is a powerful catalyst that can transform us and our relationships. When we can finally admit to what we have been trying desperately to hide, we have access to more of ourselves. We allow others, finally, to see us, which honors our relationship with them. For the first time we experience what we have always longed for—to be seen, to be known.

CONTENT VS. PROCESS

This is all a little easier if we break it down a bit. Truth, we generally believe, is comprised of concrete, irrefutable facts: the earth is round; there are seven continents. This type of truth is what is in our heads. There is another type of truth, however, that has to do with our emotions. This truth is in our hearts and is at the core of our darkest fears and our deepest longings. Unless we move out of our heads and embrace what we feel in our hearts, we will not uncover the truths that need to be expressed in order to grow mature, genuine, authentic relationships with ourselves, others, and God.

> Truth is a powerful catalyst that can transform us and our relationships.

We must start by acknowledging that we live in a two-layer world. On one level there are the facts we know in our heads: I am married and have two children. I live in a house in the suburbs. On another level there are the emotions that reside in our hearts that carry the deeper truths. I am afraid of being rejected. I am angry that you do not support me. I do not feel safe.

Put another way, the head-level facts are "content," what we see and experience around us, usually on a superficial level. It is not that these factual issues are not important. Part of truth is the facts of the case. However, if we want to deepen our relationship with Christ and each other, we need to learn how to experience and express the truths of our heart.

"Process" is the heart-level truth of what's really going on, underneath the surface of the everyday events, circumstances, and conflicts that flare up periodically. We've all seen those pictures or diagrams of an iceberg: The tip is all we can see, but there is a far larger mass below the surface. Process focuses on what is submerged. It allows us to get beyond what is visible to what is lurking beneath.

FACTS VS. FEELINGS

Michael and Diane came to counseling because it seemed they were fighting over everything, from his job to her mother. After twelve years of marriage, and with two school-aged children, they were afraid that unless they found a way of breaking the cycle they would continue to drift apart.

In an early session the tension between them was palpable. It didn't take long for what was bothering them to come pouring out.

"We've been fighting the whole way over here," Diane told me, avoiding any eye contact with Michael. "It started yesterday when he was supposed to pick me up after work to go to a parent-teacher conference, and he was late—as usual."

With a loud sigh that broadcast his annoyance that Diane was bringing this up again, Michael explained, "I was ten minutes late. Traffic was tied up on the highway. There was an accident that messed everything up."

"You were twenty minutes late," Diane interrupted. "And I just stood there, waiting, and we ended up being late for the parent-teacher conference."

"We got there five minutes late, and it was fine," Michael retorted. "I don't know why you keep bringing this up."

As I listened to Michael and Diane, I knew that pursuing the truth on the "head level"—the content—would focus on whether Michael was ten, thirteen, seventeen, or however many minutes late, and whether or not they were still able to have a productive meeting with the teacher at the scheduled appointment. These were the facts of the case, but they did not comprise the deeper truth in the context of their relationship with each other—the process.

At this point, neither Michael nor Diane was telling the deeper truth—that is, what they were feeling. To allow that deeper, relational truth to emerge, they had to be willing to examine their emotions to discover what was happening on the "heart level." Only by plumbing the depths of their emotions could they discover how they were really feeling and what was hiding underneath the anger that they displayed toward each other—and why.

Working with the couple, I asked each of them to identify how they were feeling. Their answers told me instantly where they were.

"I feel like I'm invisible half the time," Diane said.

As soon as I heard "I feel like I'm..." I knew she was moving toward a content-based answer as a strategy to protect her from the more vulnerable truth in her heart. Rather than go into her own heart, Diane was staying in her head where she could think and rationally discuss the incident of Michael being late.

When I asked Michael the same question, he didn't even try to answer with a feeling.

"I'm just doing my best. I work all day—which is harder and harder these days—and then I get stuck in traffic, and suddenly I'm the bad guy." He didn't try to throw in even a token feeling (how like us men!). Instead, he just went to pure defensiveness and rationalization.

It took a while and quite a bit of coaching on my part for Michael and Diane to learn how to get out of content and go deeper into their feelings where their more vulnerable hurts were hidden. For this, they needed some tools.

As they used them, Michael and Diane were able to break through the superficial truths, excuses, and illusions that they were using to manipulate each other and become more authentic. With genuine sharing, which required that they be honest and vulnerable with each other, Michael and Diane were able not only to stabilize their relationship, but grow in real intimacy.

THE FUNNEL OF TRUTH

The initial stage of identifying and processing our feelings is like dumping everything into a big funnel—what I call the Funnel of Truth. Everything goes in: emotional baggage, mistaken beliefs, faulty assumptions, distorted reality, rationalizations, excuses, defensiveness, even the numbness that blocks out our feelings. Slowly the parts separate as they flow through the funnel. Certain parts are siphoned off until we've reached the narrow channel at the bottom of the funnel.

As we get deeper into the truth of our heart, we move out of the facts of the case and are left with our feelings and our hungers. Instead of "You are so defensive" it is "I am so lonely and afraid I don't matter to you." What would have been "You're always late and never reliable" becomes "I was scared something had happened to you and terrified you were never coming home."

SASHET MEANS FEELINGS

To speak the language of our emotions we need to be able to identify them. Rather than take on what can be an over-whelming entire emotional spectrum, we have found it helpful at CLE to work with six families of feelings: Sad, Angry, Scared, Happy, Excited, Tender, or the acronym SASHET.

When I ask a client, "What are you feeling right now?" often what I get—particularly early on in our work—is a story or an explanation. For example, Diane said, "I feel like I'm invisible half the time," while Michael commented about how hard he worked every day.   Neither of those is a feeling. To help, I directed them to the SASHET list. Every emotion we feel falls under one of those six families of feelings, or maybe a combination of two or three.

With the list written down in front of them, I asked Diane and Michael what they were feeling.

"Irritated," Diane said, to which I replied, "Oh, you're angry."

"Yeah, I'm frustrated," Michael agreed. Again, I clarified with an observation, "So, Michael, you are feeling angry too."

Initially, both Diane and Michael were uncomfortable saying they were angry—they wanted to qualify it and, in the process, minimize their angry feelings. They were both afraid to feel angry and had the tendency to spin their feelings so that scared was "concerned," angry was "frustrated," and sad was "upset."

Observing them, however, they no longer looked as angry as they were when they first came in. There were no scowls or tense expressions; no crossed arms or clenched jaws. Simply speaking the truth about what they were feeling began to shift their experience.

Feelings repressed will fester. Feelings expressed will flourish and naturally complete themselves. Feelings expressed will lead to understanding, forgiveness, and resolution. Michael and Diane looked like they were experiencing a shift, and I wanted them to explore and express their feelings.

"What else are you feeling?" I asked them, referring to the SASHET list.

Michael glanced once and looked off into the corner. Diane studied the list, her shoulders hunched over so that she physically appeared smaller.

Finally, after some discussion and sharing, Michael and Diane broke through the content of their anger—about being late, working hard, encountering traffic, and the parent-teacher conference—to what they were feeling inside.

"I feel sad," Diane admitted. "I'm sad that we're like this. I feel hurt because I don't think you like being with me as much as you used to."

Michael looked toward her when she spoke, nodding, and

then admitted to feeling sad too. He acknowledged that at times he was afraid of Diane's anger and her hunger for closeness with him.

By focusing on SASHET, Michael and Diane went beyond their anger to identify their sadness, which was a deeper truth in the context of their relationship. This was the heart-level process of what was going on in their lives that gave such an emotional charge to being ten or twenty minutes late. Diane's deeper emotional truth was that she feared she couldn't rely on Michael to be there for her and to meet her needs. In her fear of being hurt and rejected by Michael, Diane went on the attack—criticizing him at every turn.

For Michael, the emotional truth he was hiding was his fear about his job security and that Diane wouldn't love him as much if he suddenly became unemployed. In his anger and hurt, Michael was expressing his upset indirectly, acting passive-aggressively, which is commonly experienced when people are chronically late, forgetful, and move at annoyingly slow speeds. This was confirmed when he later admitted that while there was more traffic than usual on the highway, the real issue was that he had left the office about ten minutes late.

These truths were painful for them to admit at first because neither of them felt safe. They were coming from the root of insecurities and fears that, for each of them, went all the way back to childhood. Until they could get honest on the emotional level about what they were feeling, however, they would continue to pick at each other over the "content" on the surface of their lives. Michael would continue to act out in a passive-aggressive manner, and Diane would attack and find fault over everything Michael did.

> Feelings repressed will fester. Feelings expressed will flourish and naturally complete themselves.

Locked into the content level of he said/she said and blaming, Michael and Diane had built their anger until it reached toxic levels. Only by going deep into the truth of their feelings could they reach a level of honesty where they could begin to work effectively at having a more genuine, meaningful, and mature relationship.

Even though they had been married for twelve years, Diane and Michael were both afraid of true intimacy with each other. With the hurts and wounds that came from their families of origin, Diane and Michael had tried to live together on the surface, rather than forge a deeper bond on the emotional level.

What kept them from admitting their deeper truths was their belief that there was something wrong with them and their marriage. Although they didn't express these concerns to each other, they were each worried that their marriage was inferior to the ideal that surely everyone else must be experiencing. It was only by getting honest with each other, including risking telling painful truths about themselves and each other, that Diane and Michael could begin to build the kind of marriage for which they had both hungered.

For this couple, mistakenly believing on a deep level that

they would never be loved and fulfilled no matter what they did had actually been an unconscious force that brought them together. By becoming more emotionally honest and taking the risk to explore their deeper hungers, Diane and Michael—for the first time in their marriage—had an opportunity for a genuine, meaningful, and nurturing relationship. The more they were willing to stretch outside their comfort zones to express and explore the inner truths on the emotional level, the more they could experience true intimacy.

By admitting to what they were starving for in their lives, they could begin to experience what it would be like to be fulfilled. By doing the hard work of looking at themselves and telling the truth at the heart level, they began, through their marriage, to know God in their lives on a much deeper and more genuine level, experiencing the fruits of an ever-maturing faith-filled relationship.

BEFORE THE COCK CROWS: AN UNCOMFORTABLE TRUTH

Exploring the stories of our lives at a heart level leads us to uncomfortable and often painful truths—about ourselves, our pasts, and our choices. These are the parts of ourselves that we consider to be bad and wrong, unlovable, and unacceptable. In God's eyes, however, we are loved. Jesus, who became incarnate in order to experience life and journey with us in all ways, has nothing but compassion for us. When we risk showing Him it all—our anger, fear, and sadness, our failings, faults, and brokenness—we experience the healing balm of His compassion.

Scripture has many examples of people with uncomfortable truths that were revealed, from the woman at the well who had lived with several men, none of whom were her husband, to Paul, the murderer of Christians, who was converted on the road to Damascus. Peter too—the "rock" upon which Jesus would build the church—had an uncomfortable truth, one that had been prophesied of him by Jesus but which he vehemently denied, that before the rooster crowed on the day of Jesus' arrest, Peter would deny Him three times.

The outcome seems so unlikely from where the story begins. When Judas Iscariot leads a mob that includes armed soldiers to arrest Jesus, Peter stands up to them even though he is outnumbered. Armed only with what is described as a short sword—probably not much more than a knife—Peter tries in vain to hold them off. John 18 tells how Peter draws his weapon and strikes the high priest's servant, cutting off the man's right ear.

Peter, however, is rebuked by Jesus for this show of bravado. This is no time for resisting: It's time for Jesus to surrender to His Father's will. Jesus commands Peter, "Put your sword away! Shall I not drink the cup the Father has given me?" (v. 11).

The truth—at least on a head level—is that Peter really is ready in this moment to lay down his life for Jesus, which could very well happen if Jesus does not step in. We cannot deny that Peter exhibits tremendous loyalty, love, and courage in standing up for Jesus. Later on, however, as the reality of Jesus' fate becomes clearer, Peter's courage wanes in the face of his grief and despair. Then his deeper, more vulnerable truth is revealed.

As we read in Luke 22, after Jesus has been led away to the house of the high priest, Peter follows at a distance. Standing around a fire in the courtyard, Peter is confronted by a servant girl who identifies him as one of Jesus' companions. Peter, however, denies it, saying, "Woman, I don't know him" (v. 57).

Shortly thereafter, Peter is pointed out by a second person, who says, "You also are one of them" (v. 58)

This time, Peter is indignant in his reply: "Man, I am not!" (v. 58).

An hour later, Peter is recognized again by another passerby, who says, "Certainly this fellow was with him, for he is a Galilean" (v. 59).

Now Peter is incensed. "Man, I don't know what you're talking about!" (v. 60).

As Peter utters these words, the rooster crows. And Jesus turns and looks straight at Peter, who remembers the words that have been spoken to him. "Before the rooster crows today, you will disown me three times" (v. 61)

Peter goes outside the courtyard where he had been trying to hide and weeps bitterly.

What, we have to wonder, did Peter see in Jesus' face? Disgust? Contempt? Shame? Have you ever considered that perhaps Jesus looked at Peter with tenderness, understanding, and compassion, as if to say, "You are confused, frightened, and facing despair. I know. And I understand. Everything will be OK. Trust me. This is not your fault. My Father's will must be done"? The amazing demonstration of Jesus' love, along with the dreadful loss of a friend he loved deeply, might be one part of why Peter cries with such anguish.

Peter's story encourages us to look below the surface of circumstances and appearances, and beyond the projections of perceptions and assumptions. We struggle because we want the world to view us in a particular way. We want to maintain our "false self"—the persona of being good, moral, kind, upright, and dependable people. At our core, however, our emotions belie deeper issues, from our fear of abandonment to our lack of faith. We don't like to look at these tendencies within ourselves, and we certainly don't want others to gaze on them. Unless these parts of ourselves are brought into the light, however, they will become an expanding flaw in our character, limiting our potential for intimacy in our relationships.

WOUNDS THAT SET US FREE

As we begin to explore what's going on in our lives on a deeper (process) level, we inevitably encounter our resistance and defensiveness. Defensiveness is universal. We don't like admitting our truths because it makes us feel too exposed and vulnerable—just waiting to be criticized or attacked. We get defensive even about the things that we know are true about ourselves because we don't want to admit to our faults and failings—or the deeper hungers underlying them.

Our defense mechanisms are not "bad" or "wrong." They are simply our way of dealing with threats or perceived threats— many of which we learned and have practiced since childhood. While our defenses in theory are trying to protect us from danger, they become stumbling blocks that interfere with our capacity to build and grow more authentic, meaningful, and mature relationships.

We resort to denial to keep from seeing an overwhelming problem or issue which we do not believe we can face or change. Or we project onto others our unacceptable thoughts, feelings, or motives—meaning we assign to someone else what we are really thinking or feeling ourselves.

Our deeper truths, however, bubble up within us like a wellspring. Try as we might, our secrets and mistaken beliefs—everything we think we have hidden—eventually come to light. The longer we hide our true selves, the larger the dam of shameful secrets grows and eventually begins to overflow. As soon as we begin to scratch the surface, what we hold inside begins to seep out. This is where we either hide our heads in the sand or reach out for the strength of God's grace and the light of His truth to bring what is in the dark to light. We experience the relief that comes from telling the truth, triggering the process of growth and maturity.

As part of a group exercise at CLE, Roger received feedback—all of it positive. A charismatic man, he was used to positive reactions from people. In fact, he was very skilled at manipulating people in order to be well-liked. When it came time for me to give my feedback, however, I made an observation: "This is exactly what Roger is used to in his life. He gets everyone to adore him, but they do not see him as he really is. The only person who sees the real Roger is his wife."

The next day Roger called me and lashed out in anger. His biggest complaint was that, in all our individual sessions, I had never given him this feedback. But as soon as there was an audience, as he saw it, I slapped him with negative feedback.

"Maybe you're threatened by the attention I was getting from the group," he told me.

Listening to Roger, I knew he felt vulnerable and exposed in the group session, but instead of just sitting with those feelings, he resorted to "ego repair." After turning it over and over in his mind that night, he had awakened the next morning with a carefully constructed case proving that his pain was my fault. Lashing out at me was his way of trying to shift the focus from his feelings of vulnerability to seeing me as the one to blame for his pain.

> Try as we might, our secrets and mistaken beliefs—everything we think we have hidden—eventually come to light.

By listening to Roger and not responding to his accusations, I gave him the space to experience all of his emotions: anger at first, fear, and eventually some sadness. Once his feelings were identified, we could look at his defensive strategy, which was attacking me to deflect his painful and uncomfortable feelings. This awareness opened the door for him to grasp and begin to embrace his core issues.

To explain, I used the analogy of fishing: showing him how he was using his accusations as a lure to entice someone to take the bait and engage in a fight with him—a strategy he used frequently with his wife. However, I had not taken the bait; I wanted him to follow the trail from his feelings to his defensiveness and the core issues underneath.

Roger began to acknowledge that his defensiveness hid his hunger for attention and affirmation, as well as his desire to be respected and loved. His insecurities and anxiety, however, had never let him believe he could gain acceptance by being his authentic self. In the past his only way of getting attention had been to try to look good by manipulating and managing people, which provided him a temporary drug-like high when he received positive feedback. Hearing truthful feedback from me, while uncomfortable for him, was actually what he craved.

As Roger's experience demonstrates, our defense mechanisms want to keep our issues hidden in the darkness so that no one will ever find out about the pain and trauma from our past. Nonetheless, even in the safety of our unconscious, these issues, traumas, and fears want to come out. As we begin the exploration process from surface thoughts and symptoms to defense mechanisms and eventually into our core issues, what has been hidden will begin to emerge, hinting at what lies below the surface of our conscious awareness. These hidden hurts act like scouts to help point us in the direction of the path of healing and wholeness. It is in embracing and acknowledging these wounds that we will be set free.

"TRUTH IS LOVE"

As we become aware of God's grace working in our lives, we experience a sense of humility. We focus, in Jesus' words, on the "log in our own eyes," rather than noticing the speck in someone else's (see Matthew 7:1–5). We begin to recognize that the only person we can really change is ourselves. There is no point in wasting energy worrying that other people are going to get away with something. Instead of playing prosecuting attorneys trying to build cases and win convictions, we simply need to take responsibility for transforming our lives and continuing to mature in our relationship with Christ.

Growing in grace and embracing truth, we gradually begin to expect that we will speak our truth to others and they to us. We do so with the hope that they use the feedback we provide to further their transformation into the image of their most Christlike selves. We also receive the truth in their feedback, incorporating it into our life project of becoming our most magnificent selves, created in the image of God.

We need a deep and abiding sense of grace, self-love, and self-acceptance to be able to transform, because we will only be able to make significant changes if we are getting feedback from others. We must learn to develop the emotional calluses to be able to handle the hurt and anger associated with receiving corrective feedback of others and of God. This is why grace is the cornerstone of the foundation upon which we build a vision for intimate relationships with ourselves, with others, and with God.

We are all blind to many things about ourselves and our character. We are only able to see the truth about ourselves and our blind spots with the feedback of those around us. It takes time and effort to learn how to embrace the feedback as love, instead of viewing it as hurtful criticism meant to tear down without building up. As Paul wrote in Ephesians 4:29, "Do not let any unwholesome talk come out of your mouths, but only what is helpful for building others up according to their needs, that it may benefit those who listen."

To become truth-tellers and to give and receive corrective truth about others as well as ourselves requires a purposeful commitment to wanting the best for others as well as ourselves. Jesus gave truth because He knew it was only through embracing the truth that we could be truly free, ultimately becoming transformed into the image of God in Christ.

That is the truth, and in this truth we are set free. First, however, we have to uncover the things that mark and color the truth: the ways in which we dabble in what looks like relationship but in reality is disconnection from ourselves and others. In safe and trusting environments, we slowly let down our defense mechanisms and look at ourselves as we are: magnificent, beautiful, wonderful, deserving of love and being loved, and with abundant access to the grace and healing that we desire.

Reflections on Truth

- What are the most common ways in which you defend yourself when you are feeling misunderstood, accused, or attacked? Do you deny or deflect, bluster or blame?

- How do you view the world—as a courtroom to be avoided or a playground to be enjoyed? Are there some experiences that stand out where you were shamed or punished for making mistakes?

- Replay a recent argument or misunderstanding you had with your partner or a close friend. Identify the two levels of communication that were going on: content (the facts of the case) and process (the feelings in the moment). What feelings were you experiencing? How did expressing your feelings first help you to empathize with the other person and resolve your differences?

- Are there some mistaken beliefs you may have about yourself, others, and life in general that make it difficult to feel safe in your relationships: "I am too much;" "People don't care about others;" "The world is not safe"?

- How did your experiences growing up in your family of origin influence the way you see yourself and others?

- Who are the truth-tellers in your life—the people you can trust will risk sharing hard truths with you?

Chapter 4

BEFRIENDING YOUR FEAR

*The Spirit you received does not make you slaves,
so that you live in fear again; rather, the Spirit
you received brought about your adoption to
sonship. And by him we cry, "Abba, Father"*
(ROMANS 8:15).

IT WAS A seemingly normal Saturday morning. My
son-in-law, John, was solo parenting and brought the kids
over for a visit. He was sitting with Vivienne, almost two
years old, in his lap on the deck and I was running around with
Barrett, who had just turned three. The kids were enjoying a
snack of gummy bears. Without warning, Vivienne collapsed.
We were stunned. It was like watching a balloon suddenly
deflate. In that moment I knew terror.

When I looked in Vivienne's eyes, they were vacuous, the
coloring in her face, gray. I could no longer see that young and
vibrant spirit pulsing in her body.

We immediately picked her up, thinking that she must be

choking on a gummy bear. Why else would she just collapse and stop breathing?

My heart racing, I turned Vivienne upside down with John's help and struck her on the back, attempting to dislodge any candy caught in her throat. Nothing happened. She lay there limp and lifeless. John began putting his finger down her throat hoping to find something that he could dislodge from her windpipe. No change. John and I looked at each other in shock, feeling utterly helpless. Our brains were scrambling to figure out what we could do. I had never felt more powerless.

I lost track of time, but while John's hand was in her mouth trying to sweep for obstructions Vivienne began biting it and convulsing. We heard what sounded like a cough. It was the most wonderful sound: Vivienne was alive. She was breathing again, and a measure of life began to return to her eyes. Relief washed over me. In my wildest dreams, I would never believe that I would be grateful for a child to have a seizure. She was clearly out of it and disoriented, but she was alive.

I dialed 911 and suddenly a tsunami of emotion hit me. I couldn't get the words out. The 911 operator was so calm and kind. She knew my address. She could tell in my voice that something was terribly wrong and we really needed help. She assured me that help was on the way. Eventually I was able to give her the information she needed.

In seconds we heard the sirens. Carrying Vivienne, we ran out into the street in front of our house to meet the para-medics. They quickly examined her and rushed her to the hospital. I made arrangements for Barrett's care and jumped in my car to follow. Vivienne was evaluated and transferred to a pediatric intensive care unit at another hospital. She was given all kinds of tests and was observed for several days. There never was an explanation for what happened.

John and I will never be the same. We bonded through that shared experience, much as I imagine men who have served in combat together do.

Now, every time I see Vivienne, I look deeply into her eyes, searching to reassure myself that her spirit is present. I will never again take for granted the light in her eyes.

BEFRIENDING FEAR

Fear is uncomfortable for most of us. When we experience it we often shrink back; it's a natural response. It's hard to take a step willingly toward fear, especially when there is an alternative route—even if it means retreating. Going back is often more appealing than stepping forward.

By refusing to confront our fears, however, we shut out the possibility of having a bigger life with more experiences that stretch and challenge us beyond the tidy borders of our comfort zones. Too often we submit to our fears needlessly and indulgently, keeping us small and limited. As "slaves" again to "fear," as Paul wrote in Romans 8:15, we banish ourselves to scarcity, the belief that there is not enough, instead of dwelling in abundance.

The way forward is to become comfortable with fear, befriending it. When there is a very real and imminent danger, as there was with Vivienne, the best action often comes when we heed our fears. Exploring and expressing our fear allows us to discern between a real danger and a limiting belief that may very well stem from childhood. But first, we have to feel our fear, which is something many of us have avoided doing for years.

Instead, we have become detached from our feelings. We're so shut down that we're numb inside. We can start to raise our awareness of what it means to feel a particular feeling by paying attention to the accompanying sensations in our bodies. Physical cues such as a knot in our gut, our hearts racing, or tightness somewhere in our bodies tell us what we are feeling, even when we can't register it on an emotional level.

When I was a young man, I was in such a state of denial about my feelings that I could not admit that I felt fear at all. Instead, I buried my fear by doing the exact opposite. I played sports fearlessly. When I or a teammate got hurt, I became even more aggressive. Assuming the hurt inflicted was the result of malicious intent, I responded as if I were in a life-or-death scenario; only one of us was going to win and it was going to be me. I didn't stop until I exacted revenge.

Looking back, I realize that I was scared most of the time—not in the sense of biting my nails and cowering in the corner. Rather, I experienced a sense of dread that existed at a low, but ever-present level all the time—a kind of hyper-vigilance intended to protect me from ever getting hurt again. My basic survival instincts overrode even the moral and spiritual teachings about being loved that I had learned and embraced as a new Christian.

Much of this was happening on an unconscious level. I had become so shut down to my emotions that I did not equate the churning in my gut or breaking out in a cold sweat as physical signals that I was experiencing fear. As a result, I couldn't see at the time how my outlook on life—that people were dangerous and wanted to hurt me—was affecting my relationships with others and with God. I might be able to say, "Jesus loves me," but I was still living as if God was out to get me. Deep down, I was afraid to really trust anyone, especially God.

In time, as I became more aware of my fear, my first instinct was to find out how to get rid of it. As far as I was concerned, all this fear served no purpose in my life. So I tried to make a deal with God: If I did enough personal growth work, went to enough counseling sessions, and attended enough retreats, maybe he would take away my fear. To my surprise, the exact opposite happened. The more personal growth work I did, the more conscious I became of all my feelings, including fear. The more I felt my feelings, the more alive I felt. The more alive I became, the more I felt my feelings.

My breakthrough in stopping this cycle came during a retreat in which I participated in some breathing exercises designed to encourage openness to God and my unconscious. Entering a meditative, dreamlike state, I envisioned myself walking alone through a very dark forest. The huge trees and impenetrable shadows were right out of a childhood nightmare. In my mind, as I walked deeper into the forest I suddenly became aware of something following me. My sense of terror built, much like what I remembered feeling as a kid. No longer able to contain my sense of powerlessness and feeling of despair, I started to sob. A lifetime of stored anguish poured out of me.

It was then, nearly paralyzed by my dread, that I finally saw what had been following me. Much to my surprise, I saw Jesus looking at me from behind a tree. His expression spoke of His love and concern for me. While I was walking through this dark and dangerous forest—a clear metaphor for those terrifying times in my life when I felt so exposed—Jesus had been with me all along. Knowing that Jesus had my back, I gained the courage, faith, and hope that I could go through whatever challenges would confront me in the future.

Although I can't explain what happened that day, I sensed that I was more deeply loved than I had ever felt before. As I became more open, alive, and aware, things suddenly made sense to me. Even though I had endured my fair share of very painful experiences, I had never been alone or abandoned. I was not disturbed by the question of why God had "allowed" such awful things to happen to me. Instead, I was so comforted by His presence that I could accept my sufferings as part of being human.

My faith grew that day. I experienced that God was genuinely in relationship with me. There was no need for me to try to manage and manipulate Him, or to make myself into a smaller, quieter version of who I am. God could handle all of me, including the truth of my hurt, rage, and upset. In that moment I realized how much bigger God was than whom I had imagined Him to be because of my limiting beliefs. I was not "too much" for Him, as I always feared.

In time, I was able to recognize that I'd had some terrifying experiences in my childhood. To protect myself, I had blocked out occasions on which I suffered violent physical abuse. One time in particular, I remember being hit repeatedly with a belt for swearing. I recall the terror and helplessness as I tried desperately to crawl away. It seemed like the beating would never end.

Now the time had come to open myself up to my hidden fears. As I did that, I increasingly grew in my faith and trust, and experienced deeper intimacy in mature relationships with God and others. I let grace and truth do their work. Grace created the safety net to open the wounds I had hidden for years. Truth allowed me to admit the fear, pain, and anger I had denied.

Through my insight I did not banish my fear. Rather, I began to befriend it—paying attention to what my fear was trying to tell me. Anyone who goes into danger without being afraid will not live: Fear helps keep us alive. Therefore, our goal is not to shut off fear entirely or to walk around as if we are fearless. Instead, we partner with fear as our adviser—but not the boss who runs the show. Fear's appropriate role is to let us know if there is a real threat—like jumping out of an airplane without a parachute—or just a make-believe one—the monster under the bed—that keeps us from trying something new or reaching out to people who are different.

With fear in its proper place, we build trust—in ourselves, in others, and in God. Trust is the confidence that we have the character and resources we need to overcome an obstacle, solve a problem, or face a challenge. Trust does not ensure that we will always be safe, the way that an overprotective mother keeps her child from ever having a bump or a bruise. But trust lets us know that there is a safety net underneath us, that we may fall and even get injured a bit, but we won't die. If we want to live in abundance instead of in scarcity we have to trust that the world is a safe place as we continually take more and more risks.

Learning to trust the world is a major step in our development. Doing so requires that we recognize the places where scarcity locks us into old patterns. This kind of fear stems from human survival instincts that served our ancestors well. In times of famine, preserving resources was an appropriate and life-saving response to scarcity. Today, however, scarcity is a global fear that there is not enough. It stunts our growth, keeps us small, and interferes with us having the kinds of experiences and interactions with others that foster our growth. Men often have a problem admitting fear, which they view as being unmanly. Some women too have issues with fear, which they associate with being powerless and vulnerable. Oftentimes we tell ourselves that fear is something we need to get over, as I did for so many years. Even when we bravely say that we are going to face our fears, often we only sidestep them to let the proverbial sleeping dog lie. Or else we are so numb to our feelings that we can't even feel our fear.

As a therapist, one of the places I encounter other people's fear is when I invite clients to a workshop or retreat for the first time. Even though they are hungry for such a growth opportunity, often their fear kicks in and they perceive this new experience as a threat. No matter that they will be in a safe and supportive environment. The experience itself is new and, therefore, outside their comfort zones. In response, people try to come up with rationalizations and excuses as to why they cannot participate. Then they are faced with a choice:

keeping themselves locked in scarcity or taking a risk to taste the aliveness that is part of having a fuller, more abundant life.

SCARCITY VS. THE PROMISED LAND

When we live in scarcity, a powerful belief that there is not enough or we are not enough, we exile ourselves to the desert of our fears. Leaving scarcity behind does take courage, and some of the places where we experience abundance may even look a little scary at times. But unless we are willing to cross the border into a new territory, we will never reach our promised land.

> Trust lets us know that there is a safety net underneath us, that we may fall and even get injured a bit, but we won't die.

In Numbers 13 we read how the Israelites, after wandering in the desert for two years, reached the land of Canaan. They knew that God was leading them to the Promised Land, and it seemed to Moses as if they had arrived. Before moving the Israelites in, however, Moses wanted to explore Canaan, so he sent out twelve spies on a mission to scout out what lay before them. As Moses instructed them,

"See what the land is like and whether the people who live there are strong or weak, few or many. What kind of land do they live in? Is it good or bad? What kind of towns do they live in? Are they unwalled or fortified? How is the soil? Is it fertile or poor? Are there trees on it or not? Do your best to bring back some of the fruit of the land" (v. 18–20).

With Moses' instructions the spies set out. When they reached the Valley of Eshcol, they cut off a branch bearing a single cluster of grapes so large that they had to carry it on a pole between them and gathered pomegranates and figs. At the end of forty days of exploring the land, they headed back to give their report to Moses and the whole assembly.

"We went into the land to which you sent us, and it does flow with milk and honey! Here is its fruit!" (v. 27).

If the Israelites wanted to know about the abundance of the land, there was ample evidence. But then their fear of the unknown took hold, and scarcity began to tarnish the picture.

"But the people who live there are powerful, and the cities are fortified and very large. We even saw descendants of Anak here. The Amalekites live in the Negev; the Hittites, Jebusites and Amorites live in the hill country; and the Canaanites live near the sea and along the Jordan" (vv. 28–29).

Hearing the rumbles of fear among the people, Caleb—who had been one of the men who explored the country—silenced them. As he told Moses, "We should go up and take possession of the land, for we can certainly do it" (v. 30).

Here was a man living in abundance! He had seen the "milk and honey" and the lush fruits of the earth, and he was ready to claim his share—even if it meant confronting his fears of gigantic strangers who looked, acted, and spoke differently than he. Sadly, Caleb was in the minority.

But the men who had gone up with him said, "We can't attack those people; they are stronger than we are. And they spread among the Israelites a bad report about the land they had explored. They said, 'The land we explored devours those living in it. All the people we saw there are of great size.... We seemed like grasshoppers in our own eyes, and we looked the same to them'" (vv. 31–33).

As survival instincts took over, the people chose to hide out in scarcity—the comfortable belief that playing it safe and avoiding risk is worth more than living a life of faith and adventure. They turned their back on the Promised Land of abundance and wandered for another thirty-eight years in the desert, becoming more and more dissatisfied until they openly complained that they wished they had died back in Egypt where they had been slaves.

Had the Israelites taken up the challenge right then and there, they would have faced some formidable obstacles. The people who inhabited the land were powerful and strangely different. The Israelites would have had the fight of their lives to capture the land. Using their fear to guide them, but not govern them, they could have trusted that God would not lead them into the Promised Land without the tools and capabilities to inhabit it. There may have been times when they would have felt unsafe and even threatened. But trusting themselves, each other, and God would have allowed them to move out of the desert of scarcity into a land flowing "with milk and honey." By letting their fear dominate them they chose to stay in the scarcity which was familiar.

How often do we make those same choices? We settle for crumbs in our lives because we are afraid to confront our fears that tell us that there is not enough—that we are not enough. We let that fear rule us until we have no say in our lives at all.

Confronting Our Deepest Fears

For some people, fear is rooted in the past when the world was a scary and uncertain place. For others, fears go deeper into secrets and shame that they would do anything to keep hidden. The stronger the fear, the more it keeps us from fully living our lives. Even when we are surrounded by everything we've always wanted—love, respect, accomplishment—we live in dread of the day when our secret is unveiled and everything is taken away.

To the outside world, Luke had it all: a beautiful wife, great kids, a big house, and a prestigious job that afforded him a very affluent lifestyle. Inside, however, he was in a constant state of scarcity because his fear completely overruled him. It was based in a secret shame that he harbored, one that he told me early on in our counseling relationship he was not sure if he would ever be able to share with me.

> The stronger the fear, the more it keeps us from fully living our lives.

Working with Luke, I helped him to see how his fear kept him locked in a place of scarcity where he could trust no one—not even his therapist. It took Luke a while, but finally he pushed aside the irrational beliefs that told him revealing his secret would be an emotional and relational death sentence. Luke took a powerful step of faith in abundance when he admitted to me the truth of his lifetime of sexual addiction.

Taking that first step, he experienced a sense of grace so profound it was as if he had been reborn. He radiated with aliveness as he came out of hiding and shared his secret with another person. Rather than being controlled by his fear that he would be rejected and die, he seized the life that was available to him. It was a powerful step, but only the first of many. In order to maximize the benefits of telling the truth, he couldn't stop at just sharing his secret with me. Eventually he would need to have the faith and get the support to tell his wife, trusting that she could forgive him and work to rebuild the trust in their relationship.

This was terrifying to Luke. What if she rejected him? What if she couldn't forgive him? What if she didn't love him anymore? These fears underlined the scarcity-based fears of his life telling him there was not enough grace, understanding, forgiveness, and strength in his relationship with his wife to withstand the disclosure. However, Luke also knew he would never be whole or able to have a meaningful, intimate relationship with his wife if he didn't tell the truth.

Working through his fears, Luke spent months with me preparing to tell his wife. When he did, she was obviously devastated, but their relationship did not die. Luke quickly became involved with an addiction group and, through grace, maintained abstinence—something almost unheard of in this area of addiction. His wife, knowing he had the intention and the support necessary to maintain his sexual sobriety, began in earnest to rebuild the trust in their relationship.

By facing the worst of his fears, Luke took a very powerful step toward the light of grace and truth as he embraced a life in which he could experience true abundance within himself, with his wife, and with God.

THE ABUNDANCE OF JESUS

In Jesus, we have a powerful example of living in abundance. An itinerant teacher who walked from place to place to bring the good news of God's love and forgiveness to the people, Jesus had nothing in a material sense. As He observed, "Foxes have dens and birds have nests, but the Son of Man has no place to lay his head" (Matthew 8:20). But Jesus lived abundantly in relationship to His Father and to His followers. Motivated purely by love and relationship, Jesus never let obstacles and fear-based scarcity get in His way.

In Matthew 14, Jesus had just been given the very sad news that John the Baptist, His first cousin and the prophet who had baptized Him in the Jordan, had been executed. So great was Jesus' sadness that He went off for a while by himself to a solitary place. Seeing Jesus leave by boat, the people who had followed Him all day did not disperse. Instead, they went on foot to where they knew Jesus was heading.

When Jesus landed and saw a large crowd, He had compassion on them and healed their sick.

We might imagine that, in His place, we would be annoyed with finding a crowd of people waiting for us when we came back from a much-needed time of prayer and meditation. Maybe the disciples were even whispering to Jesus at this point to tell the crowd to go home. Jesus, however, recognized the hunger and the hope of the people. He could read the fear and sadness on their faces, as well as their joy and expectation now that the teacher was among them again.

"As evening approached, the disciples came to him and said, 'This is a remote place, and it's already getting late. Send the crowds away, so they can go to the villages and buy themselves some food.'

"Jesus replied, 'They do not need to go away. You give them something to eat.'"

This was not a handful of people. The story in Matthew's gospel is called "feeding the five thousand," and in those days only the men were counted. Imagine thousands of hungry people with no provisions, and the next town a considerable distance away. In addition to being concerned that the people were hungry, the disciples may have harbored some fear about the crowd getting ugly.

Jesus, however, did not live in fear and scarcity. He relied upon the inexhaustible grace and goodness of God to provide for their needs. Even when the disciples told Him they had only five loaves of bread and two fish, Jesus was not worried. His attitude was that whatever they had would be enough.

"'Bring them here to me,' he said. And he directed the people to sit down on the grass. Taking the five loaves and the two fish and looking up to heaven, he gave thanks and broke the loaves. Then he gave them to the disciples, and the disciples gave them to the people. They all ate and were satisfied. . ." (vv. 18–20).

Trusting in God's abundance, Jesus fed that crowd with what they had. Not only that, but the leftovers filled twelve baskets! This is how God wants us to live; not in fear that we are going to subsist in near-starvation on crumbs, but with the faith and trust that we will have enough—that we are enough. God's vision for us is to live freely, expansively, and with abundance.

We will face challenges and difficulties, sorrows and loss. But we will be given the grace we need to get through it all.

To experience God's promise for us we have to put an end to fear's grip on us and our lives. Instead, we put fear in its rightful place: as a mechanism to discern the risks and the obstacles.

EXPERIENCING ALIVENESS AND ABUNDANCE

People who live in abundance are truly alive. They radiate with energy. From work to worship, they are engaged and have access to the full range of their emotions. Sustained by grace, they know they have everything they need in Christ. It's not that their lives are somehow easier or less challenging. Rather, they have become more comfortable living fully conscious of their feelings, including their fear.

Feelings may not be the best leaders, but they can be invaluable advisers. Emotionally alive and mature individuals have a partnership with all their feelings, including fear, relying on them for vital information.

Perhaps they feel some fear around pursuing a new venture, knowing that they face the possibility of failure or appearing foolish for taking a risk. Attentive to their fear, they can work through a process of principled and Spirit-led decision making. They acknowledge their fear and then decide if they should listen to its counsel, whether proceeding with caution or running from the opportunity altogether.

Sharing ourselves is risky any time. However, some people feel even more vulnerable when they communicate how they are feeling versus how they might be thinking about a particular issue. Instead of burying their ideas, creativity, and talent, spiritually mature and alive individuals express them—even though it means risking disagreement, conflict, or possibly rejection. They know that only by risking being fully themselves, including their feelings as well as their thoughts, will they be able to maximize their gifts and talents.

> Feelings may not be the best leaders, but they can be invaluable advisers.

In Matthew 25 we read the familiar parable of the talents, which actually refers to a monetary denomination. For our purposes, however, let's take the word's current-day meaning, with talents being "the abilities, qualities, and attributes that we've been given." As the parable describes, a master going on a journey entrusted his property to three servants: to one he gave five talents; to another two; and another one—"each according to his ability" (v. 15). When the master returned, the first servant who had been entrusted with five talents proudly gave them back along with five more. The servant with two talents also generated two more. The master was pleased with what they'd done, praising his good and faithful servants who had been entrusted with a little and now would be put in charge of many things.

Then the man who had been given one talent stepped up, returning only what he had been given because he buried it in the ground. "His master replied, 'You wicked, lazy servant! So you knew that I harvest where I have not sown and gather where I have not scattered seed? Well then, you should have put my money on deposit with the bankers, so that when I returned

I would have received it back with interest'" (vv. 26–27). Then he instructed the talent to be taken from the man and given to the one who had ten, stating, "For whoever has will be given more, and they will have an abundance" (v. 29).

Taking these words to heart, we get a glimpse of the life to which God calls us: taking risks, even in face of our fears, in order to invest ourselves in living lives of abundance. This is living responsibly. If we want to live in a way that pleases God we can't get away with playing it safe by doing nothing. Living so that we don't make a mistake or that we don't lose is the equivalent of hiding our talent in the ground. It is not honoring to God, and it will result in losing everything.

Aliveness allows us to take what we believe on the inside and project it out into the world in our interactions with others. We feel our feelings and take risks to connect with others, trusting in the abundance of God's grace to support us. As spiritually alive and mature individuals, we have a heightened awareness of our feelings, along with a sense of the principles and beliefs we choose to live by.

REFLECTIONS ON FEAR

- How do you know when you are experiencing fear? What happens in your body? How do you normally respond: freeze, deny and ignore, avoid and run, get angry and attack?

- In what parts of your life do you experience the most fear? Do these different fears share some common themes: "I am not safe;" "I don't fit in;" "I don't matter;" "I am alone and on my own"?

- In what areas are you letting fear hold you back from taking risks? Where have you faced your fear and risked responding in new and courageous ways?

Chapter 5

HURT AND SADNESS

Those who sow in tears will reap with songs of joy.
(PSALM 126:5).

THE DAY CHARLIE left for the Navy, I thought I would die. Being fourteen years my senior, he was more than a brother to me. He was a father figure, befriending me and playing with me, making up for what my actual father could not give me. The relationship between Dad and Charlie had always been contentious, so, for my brother, enlisting in the Navy was a way of extricating himself from a painful situation.

As a young child I could not understand what was happening or why. All I knew was that Charlie was leaving, and all his promises of seeing me again and sending me postcards meant nothing. All I knew was this aching loss I felt inside. As Charlie drove away, I stood in the driveway, waving long after his car was out of sight. I was inconsolable.

My parents understood my sadness, but to their way of thinking all this crying and carrying on had to stop. My mother, perhaps uncomfortable with her own sadness over Charlie's departure, told me to stop feeling sorry for myself. With those words, the lights went out for me inside. Without the resources to understand and process what I was feeling, I did the only thing I could: I retreated within myself. There I was safe from feeling the hurt that struck me like a physical blow and the sadness over the loss of my brother from my day-to-day life.

Over the years I added to my protective shell to guard against feeling my hurt and sadness. Better to deny those feelings, I decided, than ever be so vulnerable and exposed again. In time, I came to equate being sad with being weak and wallowing in self-pity. As a man, I saw stoicism and keeping a stiff upper lip as the way to be an adult. The irony is that by denying my hurt and sadness I was actually keeping myself locked in my childhood where I was an inconsolable five-year-old who felt abandoned. Only by opening myself up to the depth of my feelings—especially the ones that I equated with being lost, vulnerable, and exposed—could I become a fully functioning adult capable of having mature, intimate relationships with myself, with others, and with God.

BUILDING LIKE A PRESSURE COOKER

Being sad—one of the feeling groups that together with angry, scared, hurt, excited, and tender form the acronym SASHET—is a feeling of sorrow or regret. We feel sad when we experience a sense of loss, such as around the death of a loved one or the ending of a meaningful relationship. We may experience a pain in our chests: Little wonder people talk about their hearts being broken. Hurt too carries a physical sensation, but of a different variety. Hurt, which we associate with something being done to us, feels like being kicked in the gut.

Christians often try to hide their sadness out of concern that somehow it means they don't trust Jesus. We think that if we have faith, then there can be no lack in our lives—nothing at all to make us feel hurt, lost, or lonely. We also judge sadness, fearing that it means we are depressed. We don't make the distinction between sadness and the clinical diagnosis of depression. Sadness is an emotion, which we also express as being hurt, down, discouraged, despairing, or feeling hopeless. Depression is an indicator of low energy and vitality. People who are depressed often describe it as the thermostat being turned down on their lives.

We cover our sadness with anger, or become quiet and withdrawn. We may try to banish the sadness by feeling angry, which is often considered to be a more acceptable—and empowering—emotion. Anger gives us a charge, while sadness and hurt seem to diminish us instead. We may seek to soothe our hidden hurts with unhealthy behaviors such as overeating, over-sleeping, over-shopping, and other "soft addictions." Or, when dealing with pervasive or more general hurts—such as loneliness or the pain of our past—we may try to hide them so thoroughly that we do not recognize what we are feeling at all.

Sometimes we minimize our sadness out of some skewed sense of shame that we don't deserve to experience it because we don't have it as bad as someone else. This may hark back to childhood when we were told we had "nothing to complain about," or to consider the starving children in some third world country. We were told that our tears were upsetting to others, whether parents, grandparents, or siblings. Or perhaps we were warned to just stop crying or else someone would "give you something to cry about!" So we put a stopper in our tears.

But feelings unexpressed get bottled up inside, building like a pressure cooker until it lets loose—usually with a lot of drama. Afraid of being vulnerable, we may lash out at others who have hurt us. We extract an eye for an eye, making sure that they too are hurting. Or else we wallow in self-pity, which is a common ploy to get nurtured. It always backfires, however, because the support we get does not help us make the necessary changes in our lives and leaves the people around us feeling unsatisfied and resentful.

With all the baggage and propaganda surrounding sadness and hurt, it's no surprise that we have resistance to expressing these feelings. We don't want to be sad for fear of being rejected or alienated, or of making other people feel sad. Our mistaken beliefs about sadness include:

- Once I start to feel my sadness, I will never stop.
- Being sad makes me weak and vulnerable.
- Other people won't like me, because no one wants to be around someone who is down.
- Being sad just means I'm feeling sorry for myself.
- If I let you know how you've hurt me, I'll only give you ammunition to use against me in the future.

When we own our sadness, however, these mistaken beliefs

no longer have a grip on us. Staying in the moment, we express our pain, hurt, and sadness. We don't try to put up a false façade that "everything is fine." We tell the truth about our feelings. And if someone has hurt us—a spouse, a family member, or a close friend—we find the courage to express that truth responsibly: "When you said this or that I felt hurt." We avoid judgment ("You're always doing that!") or assigning motive ("I know you just want to get back at me for . . ."). Instead, we own our feelings—not the other person's.

The paradox here is that expressing our hurt and sadness in a responsible and mature way actually empowers us. Instead of exposing us to the potential for more hurt and sadness, because now people know our weak spots, expressing our feelings is a strong declaration that validates us. When we state, "I feel sad that…" or "I felt hurt when…" we are also saying, "My feelings matter. . . . I matter." Expressing our feelings is an act of self-affirmation.

> Feelings unexpressed get bottled up inside, building like a pressure cooker until it lets loose—usually with a lot of drama.

Sadness and hurt expressed lead to healing and prevent a toxic buildup from poisoning our relationships. Acknowledging what we feel, responsibly and in proportion to what is happening in the here-and-now, builds and strengthens our relationships. Sharing our feelings in the moment and working through our disagreements, misunderstandings, and upsets is not comfortable or convenient, yet it is the hallmark of mature relationships.

When we feel our sadness and hurt, we admit to ourselves and to others what we truly hunger for in the moment. These feelings, as uncomfortable as they may be, are signals that we want comfort, safety, solace. Having a pity party or getting angry at everyone else won't bring that comfort and attention. But a clear and mature expression of what we are feeling—"I feel sad . . . I am hurting . . ."—will give us the connection we long for and need.

A NEW SENSE OF POWER AND ALIVENESS

One of the most pervasive types of sadness is loneliness. This is what Nina experienced after her divorce, which also resulted in the loss of relationships with many of her friends.

Growing up, Nina had been a helpful person, a good student, the one who never caused her parents any trouble. In college she pursued a nursing degree, choosing a profession in which she focused on the needs of others. It was also during her college years that Nina put her faith in Christ and later became involved in ministry where she met her future husband, Gordon. To the outside world, theirs was a model relationship: two bright young people committed to Christ and in service to others. What the world didn't see, however, was how Nina repeatedly allowed Gordon to criticize everything that she said or did.

The couple tried counseling and Nina repeatedly sought out support from her pastor, but nothing seemed to break the cycle. Finally, after several years, Nina's pastor, at great risk to himself and his reputation as a minister, suggested that it may be time for Nina to end the relationship.

The end of a marriage is a death; a relationship has died. Nina mourned that loss, including the dashed hopes and unfulfilled dreams. The pain of that loss intensified as she began to experience the reactions of others. She was rejected by people in her church, including a surprising number of friends who sided against her. Loneliness followed as Nina was not only without her life partner, but also felt divorced from the other primary source of strength and solace in her life: her church community.

The loneliness that Nina felt after her divorce can stalk us at any age: in our youth when we don't "fit in;" as young adults when we fear we will never find "the one" for us or discover our life's passion; at mid-life with disappointments in our jobs, families, careers, relationships, and marriages; and when we are older when we have lost our sense of purpose, or feel forgotten and abandoned. Sadness of this type is more general, reflecting how we perceive the state of our lives as opposed to being triggered by a specific event.

For Nina, sadness felt like a stone lodged where her heart was. Around those who rejected her Nina's breathing was shallow, her chest tightened, her throat constricted, and her eyes ached from the tears she refused to shed in front of them. At first she tried to ignore her painful feelings by not focusing on them. But eventually, she couldn't deny the physical symptoms she was experiencing, especially the heaviness in her chest.

By admitting and expressing her feelings of sadness—loneliness, rejection, hurt, and pain—Nina could begin to move beyond them. It's not that her life suddenly turned around or that her circumstances got better. Rather, as Nina began to express her feelings—including when she confronted a former friend who had snubbed her—a new sense of power and aliveness began to radiate through her body, replacing the tightness and despair associated with holding them in.

Our pain may come on suddenly in reaction to a tragic event or unexpected loss. Greg and Jane raised four daughters in a loving Christian household. Then, one day, the second oldest was killed in a bus accident while on a missionary trip to Africa.

Hurt of this magnitude is not easily overcome. There are no easy fixes, no Hallmark-card sentiments that will make us "feel better." There is only a tremendous amount of pain and loss. Our comfort in these times can only come from relationships with others and with God. I have found that my most intimate and tender times with Christ have come following my most difficult trials of faith. This does not mean that having a relationship with God will somehow protect us from hurt or shield us from tragedy. God does not indulge or pamper His kids! But He does not leave us. Jesus, who knew pain and suffering firsthand, walks with us through every trial and moment of despair.

IN THE GARDEN OF GETHSEMANE

After the Last Supper, during which Jesus tells His twelve disciples that one of them will betray Him, the scene shifts to the Garden of Gethsemane. Matthew 26 recounts how Jesus asks the disciples to "sit here while I go over there and pray" (v. 36). He takes Peter and two of Zebedee's sons with Him. Jesus then begins to be "sorrowful and troubled" (v. 37). As Jesus says to His companions, fully and freely expressing His feelings, "My soul is overwhelmed with sorrow to the point of death. Stay here and keep watch with me" (v. 38).

Could there be any more sobering example of pain and stress? When He went in the garden before going to the cross, Jesus had full knowledge of what would soon happen to Him: "My Father, if it is possible, may this cup be taken from me. Yet not as I will, but as you will" (v. 39).

When we are hurting and in pain, this is who walks with us: the Jesus of Gethsemane who expressed the fullness of His emotions. Rather than turn away or try to numb Himself, Jesus plunged into the depths of His feelings with more aliveness than most of us can imagine. By emptying Himself into His sadness and pain, and no doubt fear as well, He became stronger to endure what His Father was asking Him to do.

As we face hard times and experience sadness, pain, and despair, we can remember what Jesus did and imitate His faith by opening ourselves up to our feelings and expressing our hearts to God in the company of our supportive community. Through the honest and vulnerable expression of our feelings—the truth of what we are experiencing—we process our pain and move forward on our journey of faith. God's ways are not our ways, and His purposes are anything but being oriented toward our comfort. God is in the business of building our character and transforming us into fully mature and developed followers of Jesus.

"Jesus Wept"

Jesus was no stranger to feelings of sadness—His own and those around Him. And on at least one occasion, He was willing to be at the center of the hurt, sadness, and anger of those around Him in order to serve a higher spiritual purpose.

As we read in John 11, Jesus' friend, Lazarus, was seriously ill. Lazarus' sisters, Mary and Martha, who were also friends of Jesus, sent word to Him. "Lord, the one you love is sick" (v. 3). No doubt these women expected Jesus to come immediately. After all, Lazarus was His dear friend, and Jesus had already gained a reputation for healing the sick far and wide. Surely He would save Lazarus. Surely He would make Lazarus a priority.

Jesus, however, did not leave right away to go see Lazarus. Instead, He stayed where He was two more days, telling His disciples, "This sickness will not end in death. No, it is for God's glory so that God's Son may be glorified through it" (v. 4). Clearly, Jesus followed no man's agenda.

By the time Jesus and the disciples arrived back in Bethany, Lazarus had already been in the tomb for four days. The scene was one of intense sadness. When Martha heard that Jesus was coming at last she ran out to meet Him, while her sister, Mary, stayed at home in the company of mourners. When Martha reached Jesus her words broadcast her sadness over her brother's death and her hurt that Jesus had done nothing to prevent it. "If you had been here, my brother would not have died," she told Him. Yet Martha held out hope: "I know that even now God will give you whatever you ask" (see vv. 21–22).

Jesus' answer was straightforward: "Your brother will rise again" (v. 23).

Whether unwilling to get her hopes up—after all, Jesus had just let her down—or uncertain of His meaning, Martha gave what we might see as a safe answer: "I know he will rise again in the resurrection on the last day" (v. 24). Her words were cerebral, demonstrating that Martha was living in her head, in the "content" of the situation, rather than in the "process" of what she was feeling.

In response, Jesus brought the issue back to the here-and-now. "I am the resurrection and the life. The one who believes in me will live, even though they die; and whoever lives by believing in me will never die. Do you believe this?" (vv. 25–26).

Martha's response was an expression of her faith in Jesus as "the Messiah, the Son of God, who is to come into the world" (v. 27). Martha then went back to the house to get Mary, telling her that Jesus was asking for her. Immediately, Mary left to see Jesus, followed by the others who had expected her to go to the tomb to mourn. Upon seeing Jesus, Mary's pain was raw: "Lord, if you had been here, my brother would not have died." Her words lacked Martha's hope and expectations. Instead, Mary was steeped in the process of her emotions, feeling and expressing only her grief.

As Mary wept, Jesus asked to be taken to where Lazarus lay. What an emotional moment this must have been for Jesus— seeing the pain of His friends, Mary and Martha, the sadness of those who mourned with them, and the bitterness of those who whispered behind His back, "Could not he who opened the eyes of the blind may have kept this man from dying?" (v. 37).

In full and open expression of His own feelings, Jesus wept.

At the tomb, Jesus asked for the stone in front of the entrance to be removed, but Martha protested, "By this time there is a bad odor, for he has been there four days" (v. 39).

Jesus replied, "Did I not tell you that if you believed, you will see the glory of God?" (v. 40).

At that, the stone was removed. Praying to His heavenly Father, Jesus thanked Him so that those who were witnesses might come to believe that God had sent Him. Then Jesus stood at the entrance of the tomb and called, "Lazarus, come out!" (v. 43). When the man emerged, his hands and feet wrapped in strips of linen and a cloth around his face, Jesus told the others, "Take off the grave clothes and let him go" (v. 44).

The story of Lazarus reveals an array of emotions—not only sadness but also anger and, in the end, joy and elation as the dead man comes back to life. What we also see is that Jesus did not instantly take away Martha's and Mary's pain and sadness, nor did He prevent it with an intervening miracle. Rather, He grieved with them—feeling His own sorrow and loss. We also see that by expressing their feelings in the moment—Martha's sadness, wrapped with anticipation that Jesus might do something after all, and Mary's pure grief—the two sisters were fully alive. They did not try to hide their feelings or cover them over with distraction and busyness. Mary, in particular, was able to feel the full depth of her sadness. Hers was the raw pain of loss without any expectation of restoration. Imagine, then, the height of her joy when her brother emerged from the tomb, restored to life.

So it is with us. The greater our capacity to feel and acknowledge our pain the more joy we will have and experience in our lives. These two emotions may be diametrically opposed, but they are also inextricably linked.

MASKING OUR FEELINGS IS LYING

The truth is that in the short run not having access to your feelings may seem to make life easier, as you swallow your upset and settle for getting along. It usually takes some time for emotional deadness to take its toll, but when it surfaces people are left facing a boatload of hurt.

By day, Carl was a highly recognized professional in his field and a sought-after athletic coach. By night, he lived a private life of loneliness and despair exacerbated by his growing dependence on alcohol. Unlike the common caricature of a professional athlete, Carl had advanced degrees in philosophy and divinity. He was a deep thinker who was an expert at keeping everyone at arm's length. When he first became a part of my men's group at CLE, Carl was virtually unaware of his feelings. The men in the group and I continually challenged him to interrupt what seemed like lectures in medieval philosophy, the content of which was way over our heads, with a few references to his feelings. We made very little headway.

Over time, it became increasingly apparent that one of the key blocks to Carl feeling his feelings was his dependence on alcohol. Most of us use our natural defenses, along with a sampling of soft addictions, to numb ourselves to our feelings.

When these no longer work and our pain starts to surface on its own, an increasing number of people turn to alcohol and drugs. We recognized Carl was never going to feel his feelings if he was numbing out to alcohol every night. Eventually, he agreed to our challenge that he attend an Alcoholics Anonymous (AA) meeting, not knowing that it would be a major step in the journey of personal transformation.

> The greater our capacity to feel and acknowledge our pain the more joy we will have and experience in our lives.

At his first AA meeting, Carl was convinced that the stories of twenty-five other men, all of whom were older than he, would have no relevance to his life. His aim was to get through the meeting so that he could come back to group having fulfilled his commitment to attend. Fortunately, his ears were opened to the men's stories that could have been his own. In that moment, he realized that alcohol was killing him and the life he longed for was on the other side of the bottle.

Getting sober was a start but not sufficient. It took the assignment of tracking his feelings, checking in with himself several times a day, and recording in a journal any time he was aware of feeling. Understanding the SASHET list of feelings opened a new perspective on life. As he began to experience his feelings, Carl became aware of the pain of the despair he had been hiding all these years. With each new round of feeling his fear, hurt, and anger Carl began to experience a new sense of hope and aliveness. By facing and feeling his long-buried emotions he was able to experience the hope of new life.

The same holds true in our other relationships. Masking our feelings or pretending that everything is okay instead of acknowledging an upset is lying. It damages our relationships as much if not more than not telling the truth about some other important piece of information. A healthy relationship requires honest communication, both emotionally and conceptually—maybe even more so where feelings are concerned.

Unless I can tell you when I'm hurt, scared, or angry and accept when you tell me the same, there is no depth of relationship. We are only two people pretending to be and feel something that we are not. Relationships are built on trust, and when we are not telling the truth about what we are feeling we are not being honest and, therefore, not trustworthy. The same holds true with our relationship with God. When we feel pain, we can acknowledge it to God—telling Him how we feel and reaching out for His grace to comfort and console us through our sorrows and losses.

WHEN PAIN IS OUR FRIEND

Physical pain is the body's signal that something is wrong. One of the first things an emergency room doctor will ask a patient is, "How much pain are you in right now?" The patient's experience of pain is part of the diagnosis. We might state, therefore, that pain has a very specific purpose as part of our healing.

Often, however, we are so indignant at having pain that we immediately want to move to blaming whoever is responsible. We are quick to round up suspects and begin the process of indicting, trying, and convicting the perpetrators. Because God is sovereign and omnipotent, surely He is the one who is the most to blame. Even if He did not "cause" our suffering, He certainly could have done something about it!

So we start down the path of righteous self-pity and indignation, wondering where God is when we need Him the most, often questioning God's love as well as His capacity to do anything about it. Author and Christian thinker Philip Yancey, in his book titled *When Life Hurts*, wrote that the greatest quandaries of faith often boil down to this question: How can God love me so much and still allow me to feel pain?

Amazingly, it was Yancey's exposure to Dr. Paul Wilson Brand's work in a leprosy hospital that taught him that pain is crucial to health and survival. Because leprosy victims cannot feel pain, they became even more ill and disabled. The disfigurements that are associated with leprosy are often caused by wounds that occur because the person with the disease doesn't know he or she is being or has been injured. The reason: Pain is not present to warn them. For instance, one leprosy victim went blind because he had no pain cells in his eyes to alert him to blink.

When we are in emotional pain we know that something is not right. We have been wounded and are in need of healing. Without the pain we might never seek out "treatment." Instead, the wounds fester and eventually lead to our undoing. How many people do you know who have been sidelined in the marathon of faith because of some perceived injustice or unfair treatment? They continue to nurse their wounds and build their cases to prove that someone else was responsible for their pain.

It is critical that we learn how to deal responsibly with our feelings so that we too do not get waylaid in our journey toward wholeness in Christ. Denial is deadly. Our unexpressed feelings, our hurts, and upsets will compound emotional interest daily and eventually overwhelm us. Rationalizing our pain or making it someone else's responsibility will only serve to reinforce our sense of victimhood. We will enter the endless loop of justifying our position by blaming others and ultimately God.

As we work toward deepening our relationship with God, we need to expand our faith by telling the truth about our feelings and our hurts. It is far better for us to ask, "Where are you, God?" when we are in pain than to pretend otherwise. God takes no pleasure when we act phony—we aren't fooling Him! The only people we are fooling are those we want to impress, trying as we may to appear more pious.

In the Psalms, David models how the honesty of pain and hurt expressed directly furthers our relationship with God. Our pretenses and cover-ups, and attempts to hide our pain for fear of appearing unfaithful, only serve to distance us from God—thereby perpetuating the sense of abandonment that we fear in the first place.

Often we deny our feelings so that we can appear more spiritual, unfazed by the pain of suffering, but in the end actually become unfaithful because we have distanced ourselves from God and made ourselves disingenuous. In an attempt to do what we thought was "spiritual," we miss the fact that God intended for us to operate naturally—and it is natural to express our pain when we are hurt, much like a baby does. No one needs to teach a child to cry when he or she feels hurt, angry, or scared.

> Our pretenses and cover-ups, and attempts to hide our pain for fear of appearing unfaithful, only serve to distance us from God.

Interestingly enough, Jesus said that the truly faithful—those who are spiritually mature—must become like children in order to enter the kingdom of heaven. When a child is hurt, he cries. When she is angry or scared, she expresses herself clearly. This is an overlooked truth of how mature and faithful followers of Jesus must rediscover how to become emotionally honest and alive, expressing themselves fully in the moment.

The clear, responsible expression of our sadness—or any emotions, for that matter—clears the air. It brings to mind what Sue and I experienced in Colorado one summer when we were newlyweds. We were staying on the campus at Colorado State University, located at the foot of the Rockies, where every day, it seemed, a rainstorm was unleashed for seven or eight minutes with drops the size of quarters. And then, just as quickly as the storm gathered, it dissipated. Afterwards, the sun came out and the whole world seemed cleansed and renewed.

That image has stayed with me for years, and I often recall it when I think of those moments when our sadness is unleashed and expressed. Afterwards, we feel cleansed and renewed. Expressing our feelings, we affirm our sense of being human and thereby demonstrate respect for ourselves and for others. As we are able to feel our feelings and become more fluent in our expression of them, we are better equipped to enter into and maintain our relationships.

REFLECTIONS ON SADNESS AND HURT

- How aware are you of your feelings in difficult moments? What percentage of the time are you in touch with your emotions?

- Take a few moments right now to practice consciously asking yourself what you are feeling. Can you identify the faulty beliefs and judgments you have about painful feelings like sad, angry, scared, and hurt?

- What happens when you bottle up your feelings? In what ways do they leak out?

- With whom in your support network do you feel safe enough to share your deepest and most heartfelt feelings and thoughts?

- Recall one of your most sad and painful moments. Journal your thoughts and feelings. What happened? How did you feel?

- Are there some aspects of your life where you have been resisting expressing or talking about your feelings? If so, consider reaching out to a trusted friend with whom you can begin to share. Or you might start by journaling privately, giving yourself permission to express freely what is inside.

Chapter 6

ANGER AND ALIVENESS

Jesus turned and said to Peter, "Get behind me,
Satan! You are a stumbling block to me . . ."
(MATTHEW 16:23).

I T WAS THE day after our daughter Lauren's wedding. There had been our fair share of complications and near crises, yet, at the end of the day, we all felt it was a huge success. Lauren felt loved, honored, and celebrated. Now, the following day, we were recuperating with friends and family. We had decided to all go out to dinner with my family, my folks, and one of my wife's longtime friends, Ann.

Everything was going along smoothly until Ann inadvertently stepped on one of the Blue family landmines. She made the ill-advised decision to interrupt my dad several times while he was telling a story. I knew that Ann meant nothing by her interruptions. But my father was not the kind of easygoing guy who could deal with her manic-like antics. My stomach clenched the millisecond after Ann's first interruption, and I braced myself for the inevitable backlash.

I was watching an internal slide show of past dinners and family gatherings, where Dad had melted down after being interrupted by my mother. I was reliving the glare, the heavy breathing, and the predictable avalanche of revenge and retribution. After several of Ann's drive-by type interruptions, my father, beyond the boiling point, blew. Even now, I don't remember what he said, but I know it was awful. I was embarrassed and mortified by the missile he fired at Sue's friend.

This was one of those moments where I realized that I was now the parent and the adult—and the host. I would no longer sit back, pretend I hadn't heard, and let myself or my guests be victimized by my father's anger. My father was in his mid-eighties and experiencing the side effects of years of excessive drinking. He was acting like a petulant child, he needed some direction, and I was the one responsible for dealing with him directly and powerfully.

I got up from the table and announced that my parents and I would be leaving. As we walked to the car, I told them that Dad had embarrassed me and disrespected my guest; we were going back to the hotel and were going to have a serious discussion about what had just happened. I declared that this kind of attack would never happen again. In that moment, I realized that I was experiencing the hurt and anger associated with a lifetime of intimidation and abuse.

It was a turning point in our relationship. By facing my fear and asserting my anger powerfully and responsibly, I had faced Goliath and prevailed. I assumed the mantle of leadership and began providing the truth-telling and direction that our family had needed for years. Eventually, during what turned out to be three hours of person-to-person, authentic, and truthful feedback, my father accepted my rebuke and apologized for his outburst of anger.

This now is actually one of my sweetest memories of my relationship with my parents. I was so moved when I saw my father finally let down his guard and relinquish his defensiveness. For one of the first times I saw how hurt and scared he was underneath his rage. My dad had never learned how to integrate his anger and reactivity in the service of getting his needs met. He was just another human being who needed help learning how to harness his anger and assert his will responsibly.

FULLY ALIVE, AUTHENTIC—AND ANGRY

Anger can be an uncomfortable emotion. Because of the way we were raised, we perceive it as hurtful, mean, abusive, even dangerous. Recalling Paul's advice in Colossians 3:8 to "rid yourselves of such things as these: anger, rage, malice, slander, and filthy language from your lips," we may even regard anger as being morally wrong.

Although I agree with the spirit of Paul's teaching, I suggest that anger, in and of itself, is not the problem. Only when anger is used irresponsibly—to bully and belittle, or to abuse others—does it become an issue. I view anger as a helpful emotion because of what it tells us: that we are upset, that something we've encountered is unfair, that we need to stand up for ourselves. Anger is often the "front man" for emotions that we try to hide: fear, hurt, sadness....

Our beliefs around anger come from our families of origin

and our early childhood experiences. The message we heard over and over, most likely, was not to be angry. Anger hurts people. Anger results in being cut off from others. Anger gets you in trouble. Anger isn't allowed—or perhaps anger is okay for adults, but not for children.

As the story about my father's anger suggests, I had accumulated many judgments about anger. My dad's dangerous temper had flared up occasionally like that throughout my life. You never wanted to be around him when he was about to blow. My mother was angry too; however, hers was camouflaged and came out indirectly. Nevertheless, you knew when you had been stung by her anger. Dad's rage, though, was like the charge of a bull elephant.

In response to both, I vowed to avoid situations and confrontations before they got out of hand. As for my own anger, I pushed it down, out of sight and into the numb places inside me. Over the years, I learned to use humor, especially the self-deprecating variety, to defuse tense situations. If I couldn't get out of a confrontation, then I relied on my physical size and strength to intimidate the other person into backing down. The only place where I could fully access my anger at all was on the football field, playing fiercely and punishing anyone who wronged me or a teammate.

The problem was that by keeping such a tight rein on my feelings in hopes of appearing more rational, even-tempered, and likeable than my father, I made myself numb. By denying my feelings of anger, or trying to stuff them away, I cut myself off from essential information about myself and my interactions with others.

I did not know at the time that feelings ground us. They provide important information about what is happening within us. If our goal is to become more Christlike—fully alive, authentic, truthful, and present in the moment—then we need full access to all our feelings as well as our thoughts. And that includes our anger. Only when we feel our feelings

> Anger is often the "front man" for emotions that we try to hide: fear, hurt, sadness....

and express them to others can we experience life on a much deeper and more meaningful level.

All feelings are gifts from God to help us live to the fullest. None are "bad" or "wrong." Being angry, sad, or scared is just as acceptable and as important as feeling happy, excited, and tender. Just like the pilot of an airplane must pay attention to all the instruments and gauges, we need to rely on the full SASHET spectrum to know how we are doing.

To become spiritually mature followers of Christ we must learn how to experience our anger and express it in such a way that empowers us and deepens our relationships. There is great risk to ourselves and others when we stifle our anger.

Unexpressed, it builds until we are like volcanoes, ready to explode. In contrast, anger that's recognized, processed, and then expressed in a responsible and mature way clears the air and opens the lines of communication with our spouse, family members, friends, and associates—and also with God. Only by admitting to ourselves and others, including God, when we are angry can we reach a level of comfort and genuineness that leads to true intimacy.

HEALING ANGER

When we know how to access and use it, anger can help us diagnose when something is wrong and has upset us. It can pinpoint the source of the upset and empower us to express our feelings to the one who has caused it. This type of anger heals rather than hurts.

I had been in group counseling for nearly a year and was learning how to recognize and deal with anger. After our sessions, I joined the group as we went out for coffee to talk some more and debrief. One night we left the session together and walked to the elevator as usual. When it arrived, however, there were already people inside. Wanting to be a gentleman, I stepped aside to let everyone else in the group on the elevator first and then I wedged myself into the remaining space. As the doors closed, I heard one of the men in the group say, "Whoa, do you think the weight limit can handle this big guy?"

He was older than most of us and regarded as one of the more powerful people in the group. He was intimidating—and knew it.

I didn't respond to his comment right away. But riding down those twenty-two floors to street level I had plenty of time to decide whether I was going to take it—maybe make a little joke at my expense—or whether it was time to draw a line in the sand. Something in me shifted. I was angry, and I knew it. Rather than follow my old patterns of pushing down my feelings, trying to laugh it off so that others would like me, or harboring a secret grudge while pretending that everything was fine, I needed to address my feelings.

When we got off the elevator, I called the guy aside. A second later I was in his face, telling him that I didn't appreciate what he had said and that he had better not try to embarrass me again. As he acknowledged the truth in what I said, I sensed that he had really felt my anger and respected it. As for me, instead of feeling wounded once again, I felt victory and a newfound sense of self-respect. I didn't have a grudge to bear and a thirst for revenge crying out to be satisfied. With the air cleared, he and I joined the others for coffee.

As I reflected on the encounter, I realized that, like many Christians, I had been conditioned to avoid anger at all costs. I was very unaccustomed to mixing it up with those who were more verbally aggressive. That confrontation was a helpful step in learning how to use my anger both effectively and responsibly.

As I experienced that night, anger is a potent emotion that triggers our "fight or flight" survival response. I compare anger to the horsepower of an engine. In the New Testament, the Greek word dynamis is often translated as "force, might, strength, and miraculous power." The root of the word dynamis means "to be able, to have power." Often the power of anger is misused and abused, which is what the New Testament passages warning against anger's excesses refer to. However, the emotional power of anger can work for good in our lives and our relationships.

JESUS' ANGER AND INTIMACY

As the Scriptures show us, Jesus had no problem being angry.
The most often used example, of course, is when He drove the
money changers out of the temple. Even if we're squeamish
about anger, we accept this episode because, after all, Jesus
was standing up for the temple as a holy place—His Father's
house.

I suggest that we look for other examples when Jesus felt
His anger in the moment, when He used it directly to correct
others and invite them into a more honest and mature relationship with Him.

One of the most powerful stories about anger is found in
the gospels of Matthew and Mark, when Jesus explained to
His disciples that He must go to Jerusalem and what would
come to pass when He got there: "Jesus began to explain to His
disciples that he must go to Jerusalem and suffer many things
at the hands of the elders, the chief priests and the teachers
of the law, and that he must be killed and on the third day be
raised to life" (Matthew 16:21).

When Peter heard what Jesus said, he simply couldn't accept
this fate for Jesus, his friend and teacher, whom he loved.
"'Never, Lord!' he said. 'This shall never happen to you!'" (v.
22).

If we think about what triggered Peter's outburst as we
study the account in Matthew we see that he was upset at
the thought that Jesus would suffer and die. Consciously, he
was afraid for Jesus—and yet, more accurately he was afraid
for himself and the other disciples as well. Rather than own
up to his fear and sadness, Peter lashed out with a rebuke to

116

Jesus. Jesus' reaction was instantaneous. He needed to get Peter back on track and fast. Too much was at stake—especially Jesus' need to accept willingly the sacrifice that He was being asked by the Father to make—for anyone to go against His mission.

Turning to Peter He said sharply, "Get behind me, Satan! You are a stumbling block to me; you do not have in mind the concerns of God, but merely human concerns" (v. 23).

Peter must have felt the sting of those words. Of all the disciples, Peter may have been the closest to Jesus. Just a moment before this exchange, Peter had declared Jesus to be "the Messiah, the Son of the living God" (v. 16). Jesus had praised him, saying, "Blessed are you, Simon son of Jonah, for this was not revealed to you by flesh and blood, but by my Father in heaven" (v. 17).

Now, Jesus was so angry with Peter that He gave him a harsh verbal pushback: "Get behind me, Satan!" No doubt that retort brought Peter around quickly, like a splash of cold water. Jesus used His anger responsibly and in a straightforward manner. He did not berate Peter for every little thing that had happened between them over the previous months. Rather, Jesus needed Peter and the other disciples to hear what He was saying about going to Jerusalem, about what He would have to endure, and their role in supporting Him if they could stand up to the challenge. Jesus needed to count on Peter as a leader to be there for Him in the dark days ahead.

As Jesus told the disciples, "Whoever wants to be my disciple must deny themselves and take up their cross and follow me.

For whoever wants to save their life will lose it, but whoever loses their life will find it..." (vv. 24–25).

The intensity of Jesus' anger is a reflection of the level of intimacy he had with Peter. He was comfortable enough in their relationship that he didn't have to manage or massage His words. Jesus was clear and direct with him. He spoke freely, expressing His anger that Peter had said something that could sway him from the things of God.

Perhaps Jesus spoke so sharply because Peter's words, "This shall never happen to you," struck a chord within Him. Perhaps in His humanity Jesus really did have a hunger inside tempting Him to stay with His friends instead of facing what awaited Him in Jerusalem. Knowing that this is what He would have to go through, Jesus needed Peter—His friend, His disciple—to be the "rock," as his name implies, to support Him in moving toward the cross instead of giving in to his own fear and running away from it.

As the story of Peter and Jesus illustrates, anger is part of every healthy relationship that is going somewhere, including our relationship with God. By owning the fact that we are angry at someone, or accepting that they are angry with us, we deepen our connection with each other by being honest and genuine.

ANGER OPENS THE DOOR TO DEEPER CONNECTION

Ned and Laura had been married for eight years and had two young children when they started seeing me for counseling. Speaking to them separately, it was clear that there were obvious differences between them, particularly when it came to their ability to feel and process their emotions.

Laura was the more emotionally fluent of the two, more aware of what she was feeling—particularly anger—and had no trouble expressing it. From her point of view, the most frequent source of her upset was Ned and his laziness, unreliability, and unwillingness to keep commitments and hold up his end of the relationship. As Laura saw it, Ned didn't follow through with what he promised to do, whether picking the kids up after school or coming home at a certain time. Ned's unreliability showed that he did not love her, she concluded.

Cut off from his feelings, Ned seemed perplexed that Laura was mad at him all the time. From his perspective she was picking on him—constantly criticizing him, yelling about everything. It seemed that she was determined to find fault with everything he did. Ned felt like a victim. He came to believe that Laura was irrational and unreasonable.

Although it might seem that this couple needed more peace and tranquility and less emotional upset, Ned and Laura were stuck. I knew they loved each other. The problem was their inability to be conscious of what they were feeling and thinking in the moment, and their unwillingness to communicate responsibly with each other. Unless they could open up to each other and honestly express their feelings in the moment, there was no way they could experience healing in their marriage or greater intimacy and wholeness as spiritually healthy Christians. To help this couple repair and deepen their relationship, I had to begin by helping them feel and express the full range of their emotions, including their anger.

Typically when I work with clients, I hear one of two stories. The first is the chronicle of what someone has done to them—

> By owning the fact that we are angry at someone, or accepting that they are angry with us, we deepen our connection with each other.

whether a boss, family member, spouse, or someone else. This is the "victim" perspective: "I can't believe how unfair and critical this person is of me." The second type of story is when people talk about what another person is feeling, instead of expressing their own emotions. This is the "mind reader" perspective— life from the point of view of the co-dependent who knows another's feelings better than his or her own: "My wife is angry at me all the time." When we reference what another thinks or feels more than simply expressing what is going on for us in the moment, we are off balance.

At first, my job is to listen and to empathize. Later, as we build trust and rapport, I put my focus on helping clients shift from being stuck, usually in one of three roles. We work on getting each person to share what they feel and want instead of spending so much of their energy reacting to their partner.

For Ned and Laura, counseling sessions provided objectivity that shifted away from the story of who did what into what each was feeling. Laura was already aware of her feelings of anger but there were others underneath, especially fear and sadness. At first Ned could see only that he was feeling hurt, that he was a victim of Laura's outbursts of anger. By focusing on his feelings, however, he began to discover that not only did he feel hurt and sad in reaction to the things Laura said, but he also had a great deal of anger of his own. Unexpressed anger is toxic, particularly between two people who are supposed to be in close relationship.

Unlike Laura, who could express her anger directly, Ned took an indirect approach. He acted out in passive-aggressive ways which, as he learned through the process of counseling, were his way of retaliating against Laura and punishing her. If their marriage was to have any hope of surviving and growing, they both needed to become honest with themselves and with each other about what they were feeling and wanting from each other. To do that, they both needed to look at their core beliefs about their emotions, especially anger.

Laura had grown up in a boisterous family in which people spoke with passion and conviction. They had no rules when it came to censuring emotions. In fact, the stronger the emotions the more likely someone was to get his or her needs met. For Laura, therefore, when something bothered her there was no filter between what she felt and what she said. When something Ned did infuriated her, she let him have it and thought nothing of it.

Ned's family was far more covert and subdued. Both parents valued calmness and discouraged any open displays of strong emotions. Hence, Ned learned to bury his feelings to the point that he wasn't consciously aware of them much of the time.

For people like Ned, recognizing their emotions is difficult. In these instances I help people to associate particular physical sensations with an emotion in order for them to begin identifying what they are feeling. Anger feels like fire within. Your heart races and your blood pressure rises. Your body and especially your hands clench. Your voice becomes louder. You experience a rush of adrenaline or a jolt like electricity. In fact, many people who are more comfortable with anger have an easier time expressing it because it makes them feel powerful.

Anger is usually in response to something you do not like or do not want. With awareness, when your anger is triggered you are being provided with valuable information about your likes and dislikes. Let's take a simple example: Someone speaks to you in what you perceive to be a harsh tone of voice. Your reaction is anger. What that tells you is that you dislike the way this person is speaking to you. This feeling is also linked to a judgment that you've made; for example, that the person is looking down on you, doesn't like or respect you, or thinks you are stupid.

For many of us, this kind of emotional forensic work is uncomfortable. We'd rather be angry and leave it at that than look behind the scenes. By examining what has triggered our anger, however, we are able to get some perspective on what is really going on below the surface and get to know ourselves better. Once we have perspective we may become empowered to speak up to another person, responsibly expressing our feelings in the moment with clarity.

Honest and genuine expression of feeling in response to a trigger opens the door to deeper connection and more authentic and meaningful relationship. We no longer stay in the isolation that comes from being cut off from our feelings or pushing them below the surface where resentment builds.

This is the paradox of expressing our anger. Rather than damaging our relationships, we actually draw closer to others as we become more honest about our feelings.

THE PEANUT BUTTER EMOTION

What makes anger such a unique emotion is that it often overpowers everything, including other feelings below the surface. For that reason, I call anger the "peanut butter emotion." If you get angry enough, that's all you will feel—the same way that if you put enough peanut butter on anything (including an onion!) that's all you will taste.

For Laura, accessing her anger was not the issue. What was more challenging was to recognize that it wasn't the only emotion she was feeling. She also felt sad and hurt, although she was not aware of it because of the intensity of her anger.

When I asked how she felt when Ned was late and didn't call, her first response was that she was angry. Her facial expression and body language certainly broadcast it, but I suspected there was something else there too. When I asked Laura to describe the physical sensations she was experiencing, in addition to the adrenaline rush of her anger, she mentioned heaviness in her heart. As we worked together, she was able to put words with that feeling: sadness and a sense of despair.

It was such a breakthrough for Laura to admit that she felt genuinely sad over what was happening in her marriage and hurt that she couldn't count on Ned. As soon as Laura recognized her sadness, her demeanor changed. She lowered her voice, and her mannerisms became less animated. She choked up a couple of times as she spoke, and her eyes watered. Laura no longer needed her anger, which she could so easily access, to protect her from feeling vulnerable. Dropping her guard, she could acknowledge her hurt and sadness.

The next step was for Laura to express her sadness to Ned. "I feel hurt and sad when you don't call to tell me you are going to be late, or when you promise to do something and you don't," she told her husband. "My feelings get hurt because I fear that I'm not important to you." Hearing Laura, Ned's defenses softened and he was willing to admit his own anger and sadness. Instead of falling into their old pattern of Laura's outbursts and Ned's victimhood and passive-aggressive-ness, talking about their feelings enabled them to establish a deeper connection than they had experienced in all their years together.

For his part during our work together, Ned began to admit that he was very angry at Laura and did not like how he responded to her, which was connected with the fact he had never learned to be comfortable expressing his own anger responsibly. As Ned began to understand his own feelings and behaviors, he saw that he had a hand in the dynamic of their relationship. It wasn't just that Laura was mad at him all the time, as he first told me. He was making her pay as well by goading her into anger with withdrawing, passive-aggressive behavior.

You Always Get What You Want

Exploring our emotions as Laura and Ned did helps us to embrace our responsibility in the situations that confront us. As we become more spiritually and emotionally mature, we stop playing the victim and responding defensively to any corrective feedback. We see that the outcomes we get reflect our intention, even if we were not conscious of what we wanted. This type of response requires a mature sense of self and a vision to transform your life through listening to the truth from other people's perspectives. Now you can see everyone as a source of truth instead of as a threat to your false self.

Until their work in counseling, Ned could never admit that he deeply resented Laura for hurting him and often wanted to punish her. Similarly, Laura was unable to acknowledge that she was drawn to Ned because he felt safe. He wasn't overpowering like the men in her family; instead, he acted more like a young man, which meant she could manipulate him more easily—but the cost to her was that he resisted and resented her much like a teenager who continually acts out.

Mutually agreeing to the outcome of trust and intimacy that they wanted to experience in their marriage, Ned and Laura committed to act accordingly. They began by accepting full responsibility for creating the mess their marriage was in. For Laura, this meant not taking the bait every time Ned—consciously or unconsciously—tried to upset her by being passive-aggressive. Instead, when he broke a commitment such as forgetting to call, she reminded him of their agreement, and expressed her hurt, sadness, and anger. Laura avoided dredging up the past or building a case against Ned and refrained from saying things such as, "You did it again. As usual, you forgot to call. You never do what you say you are going to do."

Ned also understood what would make Laura happy—

not flowers or jewelry, which she saw as only apologies and appeasements. In order to speak her "love language," he had to come through on his commitments and demonstrate his reliability. Calling her to say he was on his way to pick up the kids or confirming when he was going to be home were demonstrations of his commitment, which she most wanted to see. Following through on his agreements, being responsible, and helping out around the house and with their children, meant more to her than anything else he could do.

When he did forget to call, Ned's newfound willingness to catch himself and admit to the broken agreement—"I promised to call you if I was going to be late; I forgot, but I'm on my way home now, and we'll talk more when I get there"—helped rebuild trust and establish harmony in their marriage.

The process was not automatic at first. Because their pattern of interaction had become so ingrained they had to be very deliberate in how they acted and spoke with each other, constantly reorienting to the outcome they desired. The more emotionally engaged they became, the more their marriage healed and deepened with true intimacy between them. And so too did their spiritual lives.

GOD LOVES ALIVENESS

The state of our human relationships reflects our connection with God. If we cannot be honest about our feelings with our spouse or others who are close to us, we will not have the same openness with God. If we are distant with God, we cannot have real intimacy with our spouse.

Not only are the two relationships reflective of each other, but work on and improvement in one benefits the other. As our relationship with our spouse grows and deepens, our connection with God becomes more genuine and spontaneous. And as we feel ourselves becoming closer to God, our human relationships enjoy the fruits of our labors.

> If we cannot be honest about our feelings with our spouse or others who are close to us, we will not have the same openness with God.

By working on their marriage, Ned and Laura were also able to embrace the vision of having a personal relationship with God. Previously, their spiritual lives centered on obligation and activity: making sure the children went to church regularly and working on various committees and projects. Neither of them, however, experienced any sense of personal intimacy in their relationship with God.

Although he was very active in his church, Ned was always trying to appease God. Because he blamed early disappointments in his life on God, Ned feared making Him angry, and so he tried to avoid God's wrath by doing good works. What he was actually doing was trying to manipulate God by trying to earn His favor. It was no surprise to learn that Ned had engaged in the same pattern of interaction with his father.

Laura had struggled with her faith over the years. She felt that God had been unfair because her mother died when Laura was only a teenager. In her relationship with God, she engaged in her own passive-aggressive behavior: refusing to go to church as a way of punishing God and protesting against Him, for example. She could not bring herself to express her anger directly at God, which would have been far healthier and more spiritually mature. Instead, she tried to ignore Him.

As Ned and Laura became more honest with each other and openly expressed their feelings, including anger, their spiritual lives deepened. As they became more authentic, being more honest with God about all that they were feeling, worship became more meaningful, and they began to pray as a couple, with spontaneous expressions of their thoughts and feelings to God.

Spiritual maturity requires that we acknowledge what we feel in the moment. Instead of acting out we bring our full selves into our relationships with each other and with God. Refusing to pretend we are something we're not, or that we aren't feeling certain emotions such as anger, sadness, hurt, and fear, we recognize that God wants our honesty and candor.

As we see in Jesus' interactions with others, God loves aliveness. He wants us to use all our feelings. Why else would we be equipped with such an emotional range? God gave us these tools to deepen our awareness and build relationships. We are neither too much nor not enough for God. He loves us and longs to connect with us exactly where we are, to bring us into the fullness of the life of grace He has for each of us, angry and not.

REFLECTIONS ON ANGER AND ALIVENESS

- Who expressed anger in your family? In what ways did they show it?

- What are the things that trigger anger in you? Identify the top five situations or events that you feel most angry about.

- Reflect on a time when a confrontation led to a transformative experience in your development. What were you initially feeling and thinking when you were confronted? What helped you to see the truth in what they were saying?

- Focus on a recent conflict that was unsatisfying. Think through how you might revisit the encounter by expressing your feelings and acting more responsibly. Now, will you go back to the person and ask for a "re-do"?

Chapter 7

RESPONSIBILITY

*His master replied, "Well done, good and faithful
servant! You have been faithful with a few
things; I will put you in charge of many things.
Come and share your master's happiness!"*
(MATTHEW 25:21).

A FEW YEARS AGO, my father had a serious stroke at the
age of ninety-three. He had always been a very strong
man, surviving numerous illnesses including cancer,
diabetes, and alcoholism. Nothing, it seemed, could knock
him down. So when my brother Bob called me on a Tuesday
afternoon to tell me that Dad was in the hospital, my immediate reaction was that he would recover. I simply did not take
the episode that seriously.

When I called Sue to tell her what had happened, I suggested
we leave for California on the weekend to spend a few days with
Dad. By then, I thought to myself, he would probably be back
at home. My perception changed, however, when Bob called
me back a few hours later. Tests performed at the hospital

showed that Dad had suffered a catastrophic stroke. Now I knew I had to get to him as soon as I could, though I did not have any unfinished business with him. Over many years of personal growth effort I had worked through old hurts and resentments, which allowed me to love and accept my father just as he was. All I wanted was a few moments with him, to hold his hand and talk to him.

Arriving at the airport, we learned that our flight had been delayed for two hours. While we waited, Bob called me on my cell phone to tell me that Dad's condition had deteriorated further. Still convinced that I would make it there before Dad died, I asked Bob to hold the phone up to Dad's ear so I could talk to him. I assured Dad that I would be there in four or five hours. Although my father could not communicate, other than to make unintelligible sounds, I knew he heard me. Then, a while later, Bob called again as we continued to wait.

"Dad has passed," he told me.

My first response was rage. "Passed?" I thought to myself, feeling a wave of anger rip through my body. "Dad didn't pass! What is he, a car on the highway? He died. Dad is dead!"

Despite these reactionary thoughts racing through my brain, I kept up a normal conversation with Bob. I asked him how Mom was doing and told him that I'd keep him updated when I knew more about our flight departure. When I hung up the phone, however, I was immediately aware of just how much anger I felt. I was enraged and wanted to retaliate against someone for how badly I felt. The obvious target was my brother—the "messenger" of the news I had not wanted to hear.

132

Instead of acting out on impulse, however, I stayed with my feelings to gather the insight they offered. As Sue and I waited for the flight, which was delayed for several more hours, I ruminated on what I was feeling and why. I realized that my anger had nothing to do with what Bob said. Rather, I had entered into the grieving process, which was new to me. Never before had I experienced the death of someone so close. Since I was in the initial phase of grieving, my anger and sadness were understandable.

Yet there was another dynamic at work. I recognized that I also felt guilty for not being there when Dad died and jealous that Bob had been the one to be with him. I was shaming myself for being the brother who moved away instead of being like Bob, who lived near our parents.

As I untangled the knot of feelings inside me, I recognized the choice presented to me. I could be a victim and, in response, punish my brother for how I was feeling in an attempt to feel powerful again. Or I could choose responsibility, which meant feeling all of my feelings, including the ones that made me uncomfortable, and expressing them responsibly.

THE RESPONSIBILITY TRIANGLE AND CHRISTIANITY

To some, the word "responsibility" connotes tasks or duties. To others, it suggests a sense of being at fault or to blame. "Responsibility" in the context of emotions, however, means moving away from our childish behaviors of acting out when we feel sad, scared, or angry. Instead, we choose to be responsible for how we express our feelings, as I did after learning about my father's death.

This does not mean censoring or dampening the intensity of what we're feeling. It means that we see our emotions as sources of information. Not only do they tell us what we are experiencing in the moment, but also they tell us why. With this insight we can then interact with others—particularly our spouse, family members, and friends—in a more emotionally mature way, taking responsibility for our feelings rather than blaming them on someone or something else.

I draw much of my learning on the concepts of victimhood and responsibility from the Karpman Drama Triangle developed by Stephen B. Karpman, MD, and his work in transactional analysis with Eric Berne*. To illustrate the dynamic, Karpman uses an inverted triangle, with "victim" at the point on the bottom. The other two points opposite each other at the top are the "persecutor" and the "rescuer." Locked into their drama, the three personas feed off each other: the victim feeling trapped by the persecutor and turning to the rescuer for relief.

The victim's posture is "poor me. What's happening to me is everyone else's fault." Victims blame and whine, but they are also very powerful—in a negative sort of way. Victims project an almost magnetic force that invariably draws people who are going to get angry and upset with them. Persecutors are those who blame, shame, attack, criticize, and punish those who play the role of victims. To try to escape the persecutor, the victim attracts another type of person: the rescuer. Rescuers

---

* To learn more about the Karpman Drama Triangle, go to http://karpmandramatriangle.com/index.html

are those who are drawn to victims and want to play the role of the savior, the counselor, or the sympathetic helper. And so a three-sided triangle is formed, all bonded by powerful and unhealthy dynamics. The Drama Triangle interactions become more complex when victims, to get out of their self-pity, go on the attack. Their target may be the persecutor against whom they lash out to feel empowered. Or the target could be the rescuer, who is known as the "enabler" in 12-step addiction work.

What is interesting about the Drama Triangle is that both the rescuer and the persecutor reinforce the victim's stance. The enabling person who appears to be helpful and the persecutor who seems so tough are equal contributors to the drama. The persecutor and rescuer do not necessarily have to be different people. One person can switch between the roles of persecutor and rescuer quite easily.

> Victims blame and whine, but they are also very powerful—in a negative sort of way.

We can also draw upon our own inner cast of characters in the Drama Triangle. We all have an internal persecutor, the voice inside that tells us just how flawed we are, and an inner rescuer that tells us what is happening is not fair. Whether the Drama Triangle is internal or external, what keeps the polarity intact is a lack of responsibility. Put another way, the charge or emotional energy at each of the three points of the triangle comes from externalizing the responsibility for the pain or upset that we feel. When we feel like victims, we view it as somebody else's fault. As victims, we blame the persecutor for being mean and go on the attack to retaliate, and then we turn on the rescuer for not caring or being helpful enough. By moving away from blame and into responsibility, the whole game changes, as do the roles of each person around the triangle. A person who has the courage to tell the truth about a situation or condition is not a persecutor. Rather, that person is a "truth-teller." The person who stands by someone, without becoming enmeshed as a rescuer, is a "supporter." Likewise, the person who avoids becoming a victim is the "engager"—one who engages with his or her feelings and connects responsibly with others. This healthy dynamic is the Responsibility Triangle.

As Christians, we might see it in yet another light as a reflection of the Trinity. The truth-teller is the Father, who is willing to tell us what we need to know to help us abandon our self-limiting beliefs and self-defeating ways and grow into the people we are capable of becoming. The supporter is the Paraclete, the Holy Spirit, who nurtures us with tenderness, grace, and mercy that sustain us as we experience our pain, hear the truth about ourselves, and make the necessary life-transforming changes. The engager is Jesus, who in His interactions with others shows us how to feel our feelings, express them responsibly, and enter into relationships—honestly, genuinely, and authentically.

Living responsibly stretches us into new ways of thinking and acting. It is not always easy, and we will fall back into our old ways of victimhood time and again. When we feel too vulnerable or we are unable to deal with our sadness or fear, we may well act out. When this occurs we must be careful not to victimize ourselves by being too self-critical. We take responsibility for what we've said or done, make amends if necessary, and move on. No matter how often we miss the mark, our efforts become their own reward. There is no learning apart from failure.

TALENTS AND RESPONSIBILITY

One of the clearest teachings in Scripture of the principle of responsibility is the parable of the talents recorded in Matthew 25:14–30, which we considered in the previous chapter. Pleased with the efforts of the first two servants, the master rewards them, saying, "You have been faithful with a few things; I will put you in charge of many things. Come and share your master's happiness!" (v. 21).

The third servant, however, returns only what the master gave to him because all he did was bury the money in the ground. The master becomes

> There is no learning apart from failure.

angry with this servant and punishes him severely. Clearly, what has upset the master so much is the fact that the servant never even tried.

Reading into the story, we can assume that the master has some history with the three servants, which explains why each is given a different amount of money. The first two have already proved themselves to be responsible and resourceful; therefore, the master gives them five bags and two bags, respectively. The master does not burden the third servant with too much, though. Instead, he is given one bag. All he has to do is invest it in some way—even put it on deposit with the bankers. The smallest effort, we can surmise, will show the master that this man is capable of being responsible and engaged.

The third servant, however, acts out of his fear. He's afraid of the master and doesn't think he can match up to the expectations. Instead of expressing his fears responsibly—perhaps asking the other servants for advice on how to invest, for instance—he buries the money, literally putting it out of his sight. He's like a child who closes his eyes to make something "disappear."

Feeling victimized by his own choices, the third servant decides that what he's feeling is the master's fault. So he turns persecutor, blaming it all on the master as he tries to justify his actions. "I knew you were a hard man, harvesting where you have not sown and gathering where you have not scattered. So I was afraid, and went out and hid your gold in the ground" (v. 24–25).

The master, however, sees right through the third servant's victim-based charade. Because this servant fails to act with any responsibility—not investing the gold, and also not investing himself—the master punishes him. The moral of this story highlights the principle of responsibility, which challenges each of us to get out of the victimhood that keeps us small and hidden—like a bag of gold buried in the ground. Responsibility ushers us into a more conscious, engaged life in which we take what we have been given—our "talents"—and make them into even more. In every situation we have a choice.

THE SCRIPTS OF OUR OWN DRAMAS

No matter how the scenes change, we still cast ourselves in the role of the poor victim—the one who is wronged by the persecutor and must be saved by the rescuer. It may go back to childhood, when we experienced being bullied by siblings or other children, or perhaps when we felt our parents had unrealistic expectations we could not meet or did not pay enough attention to our needs. So we repeat the same old drama: acting out as the whining child to get attention, to be validated, and to get our needs met.

Sandy's drama was triggered by a forecast for some severe winter weather in the Chicago area. Meteorologists predicted the storm would hit on a Tuesday night—when one of my groups meets at the practice—just before rush hour. Several people decided to come to group despite the forecast. They did not live far and judged for themselves that the drive was not too hazardous. Sandy, however, decided to stay home and to call in instead.

When she was connected by phone to join the session remotely, Sandy could hear the voices of the other people who had decided to come in person. In her mind, these other people had won my approval by braving the storm; by staying home, however, she had displeased me. In her sadness and anger at feeling left out, and in reaction to what she projected as my disapproval, Sandy felt like a victim. The rejection she experienced took her right back to her father, who had always set high expectations that she felt she could never achieve. Cast in the role of victim once again, Sandy perceived that I was the persecutor, the cause of all her upset, because I made the observation, as the truth-teller, that she had not come in for group while many of the others had.

If Sandy had chosen responsibility, she would have owned her decision and the feelings behind it. She could have said something along the lines of "I am terrified of winter driving. I have had some bad experiences in the past, and I just don't feel safe driving tonight." Had she done that, Sandy would have demonstrated making a responsible decision for herself. Whether I was pleased or displeased would have been of no consequence. This wasn't about me—it was about Sandy feeling comfortable about her own decision.

Sandy's choice, however, was to launch into the Drama Triangle. From victim, she turned persecutor, and her target was me. In an attempt to punish and shame me, Sandy sent me an e-mail the following day in which she chastised me for not understanding how bad the weather was and demanding that I "acknowledge and respect those of us [who] did not come and called in."

In my reply, I tried to help Sandy recognize her pattern of defensive justifications, which she frequently made after the fact and in e-mails. All of the drama—her decision to stay home, the weather forecast, the snowy roads—were totally beside the point. At the heart of it was Sandy's victimhood and her attempts to guilt-trip and shame others to gain a false sense of power and control. Moreover, what was making Sandy so angry in the first place was her need to earn my approval. Had I said to her, "It's okay, Sandy. Staying home makes sense—I give you my permission," I would have been acting in an unhealthy way, as a rescuer. Although this was what Sandy thought she wanted, such enabling behavior on my part would have only furthered her victimhood.

As long as Sandy casts herself as the victim, she will remain mired in the Drama Triangle. When she begins to take responsibility for her feelings, decisions, and actions she will have a much different experience not only with others, including me, but most importantly with herself.

"Tell Me to Come to You"

Time and again, Jesus showed the disciples that instead of clinging to their victimhood and scarcity thinking there was a more empowered and spiritually mature way of thinking, acting, and relating. The disciples, like the rest of us, often fell into complaining about how hard everything was—just like the Israelites before them, who often rebelled against God and Moses because of the difficulty of their journey to the Promised Land.

This is a mistaken theology of victimhood, based on the belief that if God really loved us and supported us He would make life much easier and more comfortable. A theology of responsibility owns the reality that life is difficult, and God makes no apologies about how hard things can get at times. He does not promise to rescue us from our victimhood. Instead He says that no matter what we go through, He is with us.

Consider what happened immediately after Jesus fed the crowd of five thousand, as related in Matthew 14, which we discussed in chapter 4. After that miracle, Jesus' disciples no doubt rejoiced over the overwhelmingly loving abundance of

God. But as we read on, the joy and confidence of their faith was short-lived.

Immediately Jesus made the disciples get into the boat and go on ahead of him to the other side, while he dismissed the crowd. After he had dismissed them, he went up on a mountainside by himself to pray. Later that night, he was there alone, and the boat was already a considerable distance from land, buffeted by the waves because the wind was against it. (vv. 22–24)

Out in the boat, the disciples were in the dark and without Jesus. The strong wind, high waves, and their own fears soon got the best of them. Remember, many of the disciples were experienced fishermen who spent much of their lives on the water. This must have been a major storm to make them so afraid. In their terror they imagined all sorts of disaster scenarios.

Suddenly, the disciples spied an unlikely sight: a man walking toward them on the water. During the fourth watch of the night, "Jesus went out to them, walking on the lake. When the disciples saw him walking on the lake, they were terrified. 'It's a ghost,' they said, and cried out in fear. But Jesus immediately said to them: 'Take courage! It is I. Don't be afraid'" (vv. 26–27).

Jesus wasn't taken aback by their reaction to His walking on the water. It was completely understandable. Instead He reassured them with the truth: "It is I. Don't be afraid."

Even the sound of Jesus' voice wasn't enough to calm their fears, though. The disciples would rather doubt their eyes or believe what they saw was a ghost. Peter put Jesus up to the test. "Lord, if it's you . . . tell me to come to you on the water" (v. 28).

Jesus replied, "Come" (see v. 29).

To his credit, Peter took the challenge. Soon he was walking on the water. As long as his eyes stayed on Jesus, Peter was fine. When the wind distracted and frightened him, however, he gave into his fear and began to sink. Sure that he would drown, Peter begged Jesus to save him. All the while Peter was looking down at his "problem"—the wind-whipped waves—instead of seeing that his supporter, Jesus, was right in front of him.

Reaching out His hand, Jesus caught Peter. While He kept Peter from drowning, Jesus did not get into the drama by taking on the role of a rescuer. Jesus didn't apologize for making Peter do something difficult, nor did He comfort Peter with, "There, there. Everything's okay now. I'll take care of you." Instead, He used the opportunity to challenge Peter's lack of faith and examine where he broke down. Jesus went straight to heart of the problem: Peter let his fear get the best of him and failed to trust Jesus.

"You of little faith," He said, "why did you doubt?" (v. 31).

There was no shame. Instead, it was a valuable learning experience, allowing Peter to see firsthand how disabling his fears were, to the point of putting him in danger of drowning. While Jesus upheld Peter and kept him safe, He brought him to a higher level of understanding. It is as if Jesus was saying to Peter, "Be an adult. Acknowledge your fear and take responsibility to live by faith. Keep your eyes on me and don't get distracted by the circumstances."

With this perspective, we might wonder what would have happened if Peter, instead of yelling out, "Lord, save me," had merely acknowledged what he was feeling. His exchange with Jesus might have been something like this:

"Lord, I'm scared, walking on the water like this. The wind and the waves are huge. Help me in my unbelief."

Jesus might have replied, "I understand. You're doing fine. This is a big storm. But believe me, I and my Father are much bigger than the weather. Keep coming and keep your eyes fixed on me."

With God, everything is possible. In Him we are fully alive, engaged, and empowered. Our choice is to answer His call to step out in trust, choosing abundance and responsibility, instead of victimhood and scarcity.

GOD THE TRUTH-TELLER

At any moment we can tell whether we're enmeshed in drama or acting responsibly by how much aliveness we feel. When we allow ourselves to be victimized by circumstances, other people, or even ourselves, our level of engagement is limited. We feel small, numb, disempowered—in other words, like a victim. By contrast, we come to understand that unless we have access to our feelings, as well as our thoughts, we cannot achieve full aliveness. When we are living responsibly we embrace all of our feelings, knowing that this is what it means to be alive and truly present. We are expansive, aware, and empowered—in other words, we are engaged.

Yet no matter how much we try to live in this spirit, there will be times when we fail. Our upset seems too great, our drama and victimhood too enticing. We get scared and hurt, and our vulnerability becomes too uncomfortable. We fall back into victimhood, praying to be saved while we scan the horizon for someone else to rescue us. If that fails, we may also look for another victim lower than us on the ladder of pity with whom we can pick a fight. We seize on this opportunity to bully someone smaller than us in order to feel a false sense of power, control, and confidence, and to insulate ourselves from our hurt and fear.

Part of our spiritual maturity is to recognize that our living responsibly is a continual goal—never a destination that we reach. We are always in the process of becoming. We enter into dialogue with God, asking for the grace and truth to be able to recognize what we can control in our lives and accepting that the outcomes we experience are our responsibility.

We stop treating Him as a persecutor who causes or allows things to happen to us, or demanding that He rescue us so we don't have to do anything on our own behalf. We no longer stay emotionally arrested like the adult-child who still relies on his or her parents to do everything. No longer satisfied by being the victim, we embrace the respon-

> Part of our spiritual maturity is to recognize that our living responsibly is a continual goal— never a destination that we reach.

sibility of becoming the adult authors of our own life. Hungry for deeper connection with ourselves, with others, and with

God, we let go of our resentment and our fear, moving away from victimhood and toward a life of faith and love.

When we act more responsibly toward God, taking ownership of our own messes and the feelings that arise because of them, we are able to move into closer relationship with Him. In this place of spiritual maturity we ask God to be the truth-teller, to show us where and how we can grow, and to be the supporter, extending His love and grace to us as we go through challenges and upsets. We still face the same choices every day, in big ways and small, in all our interactions. Rather than staying upset and waiting for someone to rescue us, though, we increasingly own our feelings and take responsibility for our actions. We increasingly trust that, whatever challenges we face, God will give us the grace to sustain us.

REFLECTIONS ON RESPONSIBILITY

- In your own words, what is the principle of responsibility, and how might you apply it in a present-day circumstance?

- Which role do you most often find yourself playing in the Drama Triangle: Victim? Rescuer? Persecutor?

- Take a recent experience where you found yourself in the Drama Triangle. Identify where you were playing one of the roles (victim, persecutor, rescuer). Consider how you might have responded differently by taking responsibility for your experience ("As a victim I found myself feeling sorry for myself, and instead I chose to simply express that I felt hurt and angry.")

Chapter 8

CHOICE AND INTENTION

Everyone was filled with awe at the many wonders
and signs performed by the apostles
(ACTS 2:43).

J ANE'S GLARE PIERCED me from the across the room. The
longer she stared, the bigger grew the pit in my stomach.
I certainly didn't want to engage with her in any way. I
wished she would just ignore me. All I knew at that moment
was that this was going to hurt.

During one of the early after-session discussions when I was
participating in Bob Wright's group—we all went out after the
formal portion ended to continue without the leaders—I said
something to Jane that offended her. I wasn't aware of it at
the time, but when I arrived at group the next week, there she
was glaring at me. I was scared and uncomfortable because
I knew something was up and I didn't know what. But I also
knew that I thought she was strange. For one thing, she was
an acupuncturist, and in the eighties that was not as common
or accepted as it is today. In my mind at the time, strange and

different equated to dangerous. So I was sitting across from this woman with the dangerous glare, and she offered to speak first.

Jane immediately tore into me, spewing anger over what I had said the week before. I was mortified by her reaction, especially because I had always thought of myself as a nice guy who was sensitive to the feelings of others. To my horror, Bob seemed to be egging her on, asking her to express what she was feeling, moment to moment. Jane's anger was a flame that Bob kept fanning with the bellows, and I was in the hot seat! In the midst of this firestorm, I kept asking myself, wasn't there some ethical principle Bob was violating such as, "Do no harm"?

Not wanting to say or do anything that would make matters worse, I silently endured Jane's tirade. That's when Bob stirred her up even more by saying, "He doesn't even respect you enough to give you an answer!" There went my hopes that Jane would eventually stop, or at least run out of steam.

Yet it got even worse. Next, the men in the group started in on me. They were upset at me for allowing Jane to talk to me like that without standing up for myself: What kind of a man was I? By this point I had descended into some private hell. I couldn't see a way out, and I had no idea why I was there in the first place.

A FIRST-CLASS VICTIM

When we are in the midst of an uncomfortable situation we often feel as if life is happening to us, instead of recognizing that what we are experiencing may be the direct result of our intentions. In this situation, I definitely knew that everything was happening to me, and it definitely was unfair. I was a first-class victim. Everything was somebody else's fault: Jane's, Bob's, and the other men in the group. I could not see that I had any choice in the matter. I didn't have to sit there and take it as Jane berated me; I could stand up for myself. But that would have required me to move out of my victimhood as the persecuted one.

I was also blind to the fact that the others were scared and intimidated by me for several reasons, including that I was an evangelical Christian, which for many of them triggered feelings of being judged. When I shut down, pulled away, and refused to engage with them it just affirmed their opinion of me as aloof and superior—no matter that I was dying inside as Jane lashed out at me.

I had an effect on the people in the group, even though I could not see it and therefore was not taking any responsibility for it. Although I considered myself to be open, sensitive, and available to others, this perception was only true in the interactions in which I was in control or leading the group. As soon as things got outside of my control or understanding, I panicked and retreated within myself. No wonder the others in the group reacted so strongly to me.

I believed that I was above all this craziness, and that I was the better person for turning the other cheek. The truth, however, was that I had shut down. I could not engage with Jane because I had never learned to tap my feelings in my relationships. My anger and ability to defend myself were only accessible to me when I played aggressive sports. Keep in mind that outside of the game of football, where I could use my speed and strength to defend myself, though, I was lost and unsure of myself.

Off the playing field I either tried to manipulate as a people pleaser or else I held myself aloof and uninvolved. Given the in-your-face style of Bob's group my lack of engagement was never going to be acceptable. In order to be a fully alive and active participant in this group—and in my own life—I had some important lessons to learn about integrating my personal power into my relationships with others. I would have to learn how to experiment with my power and how to navigate relationships with truth and mutuality, and to take responsibility for my choices and their consequences.

CHOOSE FOR YOURSELVES THIS DAY WHOM YOU WILL SERVE

All of us have choices. We have been gifted by God with the power and the capacity to decide how we are going to live our lives. Even in the midst of circumstances that are not of our choosing, we have a choice in the matter: what we want to experience and how we want to show ourselves to others.

For many this requires a shift in thinking. We may consider it to be the pious and even the polite thing to preface our plans and dreams by saying, "If God wills." Too often, however, we use the concept of "God willing" to give ourselves an out. We are off the hook for what happens to us, positive or negative, because we give all the credit—and therefore all the blame—to God. A far more spiritually mature and empowering stance is to take responsibility for our lives, for our choices, and for our intentions.

As we stretch ourselves to living bigger, bolder lives, we do not need to worry about exceeding our boundaries with God or stepping on His toes. As Jesus modeled for us, life is to be lived full-out with no holds barred. We do not have to become less in order to make God—or anyone else, for that matter—feel better. God wants us to take the initiative in our lives.

> Even in the midst of circumstances that are not of our choosing, we have a choice in the matter.

Becoming spiritually mature, ours is an inter-dependent relationship with God, trusting that he will provide everything we need while we take responsibility for everything we need to do. This brings us to the essential question: What do we choose? In the Old Testament, Joshua issued the same challenge to the Israelites: "But if serving the LORD seems undesirable to you, then choose for yourselves this day whom you will serve, whether the gods your ancestors served beyond the Euphrates, or the gods of the Amorites, in whose land you are living. But as for me and my household, we will serve the LORD" (Joshua 24:15).

As spiritually alive people, pursuing greater connection in our relationships with ourselves, with others, and with God, we believe that serving the Lord requires that we become responsible and accountable for our choices. Living fuller lives as Christ-followers, we move out of reactivity and victimhood, as we discussed in the previous chapter, and become empowered. Instead of acting like victims or lashing out as persecutors, we shift out of the Drama Triangle.

A Radical Shift in Experience

Up to the point of my encounter with Jane, my experience in church and the ministry had been that it was best not to give a lot of direct feedback. Instead, we considered it our responsibility to build others up by giving encouragement and being nice.

Although I needed encouragement in my personal growth, I needed truth even more. I was in desperate need of a wake-up call to see certain things in my life—especially my inability to feel my feelings and to relate genuinely to others. These shortcomings were causing problems in my life, in my marriage, and in my work. I was completely unaware of the effect I was having on other people, so I did not take responsibility for how my words and actions affected them. To grow, I had to learn some fundamental principles of human relationships and interactions: intention and assertion.

Intention refers to the results that we expect to receive. Our intentions influence every experience of our lives, especially our effect on others. For example, let's say that someone says, "You hurt my feelings." A common response is to give a kind of apology: "I didn't intend to." In the old days, I would have thought that sufficed. I didn't mean (intend) to hurt your feelings, so I have no responsibility. Today, that thinking is no longer acceptable. I may not have been conscious about what I said or did to hurt your feelings, but I am responsible.

Intention reminds us that in all things we have choices. Even when circumstances seem beyond our control, we have choice in how we respond and experience what is happening. When we recognize our choice we can shift from the reactivity of victimhood to assertion. It is an empowering process, to be sure. As very young children, we were highly reactive: think of the "terrible twos" of toddlers. As we mature and develop, we channel our reactive energy into assertion. Instead of focusing on what we don't want, we recognize our responsibility in choosing what we do want and how we experience our lives. Exercising our will is our choice and our responsibility and also reveals our intention: What we intend, we realize.

Assertion complements intention by empowering us to say what we want, what we are all about, and what we are going for in our lives. We assert ourselves and realize that we have the power to live the lives we want. We'll encounter challenges and obstacles, to be sure, but intention and assertions keep us moving forward.

Most of us have said, at one time or another, "I hope to lose weight." Said this way, it is not much more than an observation with little intention behind it and no assertion of how we are going to get there. What if, instead, someone declared, "I'm going to lose twenty pounds in the next six months with diet and exercise." There is much more intention here. The person asserts her desire to be healthier and more physically fit by stating what she wants to do: work with a weight coach, become accountable for diet and exercise, see a nutritionist, join a gym, and so forth.

What if we apply that same principle to our relationship

with God? How would the experience of grace and truth, the foundational principles we discussed in chapters 2 and 3, transform not only what we say, but what we experience? It might sound something like this:

"I am choosing today to hold myself as whole and complete. Throughout this day when I find myself wanting to put myself down, I am going to choose to focus on the fact that God loves me—wholly, completely, and entirely."

The only way we can experience the love of God is to choose to do so and to declare our intention to be in relationship with Him, in spite of our doubts and lack of absolute certainty. The saying often used in AA is "Fake it 'til you make it."

The same goes for our connections with others, including spouses, family members, and friends. We choose relationship instead of isolation, we choose intimacy instead of distance. If we are truly committed to building open, honest, meaningful, and dynamic relationships with God and with others— remembering that all our connections are linked and each one benefits from improvement in any area—then we will not rest until we have what we have intended. Once again, outcome reflects our intentions.

THE GOD I CAME TO KNOW LOVES US UNCONDITIONALLY

My experience with Jane and the group did not magically get better. For much of the first year, I felt disconnected and fantasized about leaving the group. But I stayed. Sometimes I think it was because I was too afraid to leave. Yet at other times I recognized that I needed to work through my fear and urge to flee because I knew I was learning the skills I needed to transform my life.

At every session, Bob continued to challenge me. Sometimes as I was sharing with the others, he would do a headstand on a chair. Admittedly, this was an unconventional approach, but he was committed to do anything necessary to push my buttons and get me to harness the aggressiveness that I tried so hard to hide. When I asked him to stop these antics and respect me, he would reply in the most infuriating singsong voice, "I will respect you as much as you respect yourself."

> The only way we can experience the love of God is to choose to do so and to declare our intention to be in relationship with Him, in spite of our doubts and lack of absolute certainty.

Sometimes I would get out of my chair and yell back, but I always felt like I was posturing—and Bob knew it. He'd call me on it, telling me I was pretending to have self-respect. My willingness to try to be self-respecting was great, however, I wasn't able yet to communicate it from the core of my being. I didn't fully believe it, or believe in myself. I was slowly growing my internal self and building an authentic sense of confidence. As I learned to treat myself with respect I could then command it from others. What Bob could see, but I could not, was who I really was. He knew I was completely cut off from my personal power.

After about a year, I began to feel more comfortable and started to get a little cocky. I thought I had learned what I needed to and that it was time for me to move on. As I saw it, I didn't need the group any more.

One afternoon, in the midst of an individual counseling session with Bob, I informed him of my decision: I was giving notice and would be leaving the group. I waited until the session was about three-quarters completed to drop this bombshell. My plan was to blurt it out and then leave, with no responsibility for my relationship with Bob, with the group, or with myself. The result was a major blow-up. Bob became furious with me and started arguing. Suddenly, we were face-to-face in a shouting match that got so loud the building manager later told us there were complaints from two floors above and two floors below Bob's high-rise office.

Later, I could see that this was what I had wanted to happen. My intention was to pick a fight with Bob as a kind of test for myself. I needed to fully feel my power and express myself verbally to someone I both feared and respected. The break-through was huge. In the midst of our argument, I practiced the tactics of verbal fighting and debate that Bob, the master, had taught me. I did my best to not get sidetracked by his comments; instead I focused on making my points, expressing myself, and not giving in to my fear. Occasionally, though, some of his points got through my defenses.

"You know nothing about the principle of inclusion," he shouted at me. "You have no sense of mutuality, inclusion, or partnering."

What he said made sense. I saw that I did not have a real concept of including others and partnering with them. Before working with Bob I was much more comfortable managing people and their reactions, along with avoiding any situations where there might be disagreements. I had no experience with two adults expressing their points of view powerfully and having both parties consider the other person's point of view and orient to what was true. This was a whole new world of mutual engagement for me.

I stormed out of Bob's office with the issue unresolved on whether I was leaving the group or not, but I felt absolutely exhilarated after the most intense verbal fight of my life. At last, I had brought my football and rugby self into the arena of interpersonal relationships. Suddenly, after months of fantasizing about getting myself out of the group, I began to realize how much I had gained by being there. I had to keep fighting—pushing forward and through my fears—because I was worth it. I could see how shut down I had been most of my life, numb to my feelings and cut off from others.

I went to the group that night and reported on my fight with Bob, telling them that I had changed my mind and realized how important the group was to me. I owned my anger and admitted to myself that I wanted to be in the group for me. I was not staying just to please others and avoid conflict. This was a monumental turning point for me and in my relationship with Bob. This time I chose with intention to be part of the group because of the outcome I wanted to achieve: namely, to be more empowered, mutual, and engaged in my life and in my relationships with others.

The next big turning point was when Bob challenged me to come on a week-long men's retreat, which was the scariest thing I could imagine at the time. It is one thing to spend a few hours with people, and it's entirely another to devote a week to being with others, uncovering our wounds and exposing the areas where we operate without integrity or in bad faith.

I was terrified going into the experience, but that week changed my life. On the last night of the retreat I was able to remember some troubling and frightening experiences I'd had as a child, which I had blocked out of my memory. As a result of sharing and being with these men I felt safe in telling my story of physical abuse. It was not just that I talked about what happened. I actually spontaneously re-experienced my memories in their presence.

At last I had learned to trust others and God enough to face things that had happened to me, which previously I was unwilling to acknowledge or remember. Now it was so apparent why I had been so scared to be in a group and trust others to have my best interests at heart. It also made sense why my physical sense of power and strength was so vital to my capacity to feel safe in the world.

After that weekend and the breakthroughs I experienced, I finally made sense to my therapist. He understood why I was so defensive. I finally accessed the pain I harbored inside, which went back to my childhood. But once I tapped into my sadness, fear, and anger there was no going back to my old ways. I was exposed at last, and in my vulnerability I could open myself up to the love of Jesus as brother, friend, and Savior as I never had before.

It may seem paradoxical that I, a Christian, deepened my faith in the midst of what I perceived to be a New Age counseling practice, where the very label of "Christian" threatened others who had been wounded by judgmental church experiences in the past. At that time I had a very limited view of how God could work in my life. As a result of what I was learning in counseling, my experience of God was being stretched as I saw Him transforming me into the image of Christ through so many unexpected avenues.

As a young Christian, the Bible was central in my pursuit of a relationship with God. I learned not to trust my feelings or my own thinking; instead, I focused on mastering the Bible and learning how to properly interpret its teaching. Looking back, I wonder if my reliance on the Bible might have been a bit excessive. I think I fell into the way of the Pharisees, putting the letter of the law ahead of the spirit of the law. I believe my excessive focus on the Bible may have contributed to me becoming increasingly rigid, dogmatic, and judgmental.

My experience of Christ was very powerful, but my limited perspectives restricted my understanding of God and His work in the world. I mistakenly assumed that the ways God worked in my life were the ways He would work in other people's lives. As a result, I had a tendency to prescribe to others what they should do to grow in their spiritual maturity.

As I matured as a person so did my understanding of God. I learned that each person is on his or her own journey and is responsible to author his or her own relationship with God. Although the Bible remained central in my spiritual development, it did not mean that it must have the same importance in someone else's journey of faith. I continued—and do to this day—to benefit from my spiritual disciplines of Bible study, prayer, meditation, witnessing, and service to others. However,

I learned to be more careful to avoid being overly directive about how others should grow in their faith.

"BUT I'M JEWISH"

Reactivity draws negativity like a lightning rod. Assertion, however, is the positively charged pole that allows us to harness our power and go for what we want and need. This experience may push us out of our comfort zone at times, but each time we face the challenge we further our personal development, and we gain experience to help others when they are up against their own challenges.

I was so grateful for the experiences I had in Bob's leadership development practice when Lisa came to my practice. Although her experiences differed from mine in the details, they were very similar on the emotional level. I had met Lisa at a community program where I was a speaker promoting the elements of positive and healthy relationships. She was moved by what I said and asked if she could have my card, which read, "Center for Life Enrichment." A short while later, she called to schedule her first session with me.

In the interim there had been some changes afoot in my counseling practice. For years Bob had urged me to own the fact that I was a Christian therapist. As he saw it, by not labeling myself as such I was hiding a key value and strength that differentiated me from other therapists. And so he challenged me to declare who I was with intention: a Christian with a background in ministry who was also a practicing therapist.

By the time Lisa came in for her appointment, I was "out" as a Christian therapist. When I greeted her in the waiting room she was holding one of our new marketing brochures that described CLE as a Christian counseling center. "I think I may have made a horrible mistake," she told me. "This is a Christian practice." "So what's the problem?" I asked.

> Reactivity draws negativity like a lightning rod.

"I'm Jewish!"

I invited Lisa into my office for our meeting, assuring her that if in the end she did not feel that it was a fit, I would not charge her. I saw in her the same fear I'd had in the group all those years before: wanting to shut down and flee out of a sense of self-protection. In my case, I had come from a conservative Christian background that was anathema to the New Age counseling practice that challenged me at every turn. For Lisa, her fear was that I would try to brainwash her into converting to Christianity.

In that moment, Lisa had a choice. She could discredit everything she had heard and experienced because now she knew I was a Christian, or she could trust that I was a decent human being and a capable therapist. From the beginning, I was drawn to her ability to express her concerns. She had no trouble voicing her thoughts, feelings, and discomfort, which I considered to be very healthy. I also had to respect myself for taking the risk of inviting Lisa to be my client, since there was the possibility that she could reject me.

Drawing from my own experience, I was able to help Lisa realize that no matter what label I wore, the outcome of the counseling relationship was hers to determine. Her responsibility was to get clear about her intention and make the choices that would lead to the desired outcome. It was up to her to decide whether she could do her growth work at a Christian counseling center even though she was Jewish.

In the eight years since, Lisa has remained a client. Every once in a while some of her old fears and concerns about whether she can trust Christians are stirred up. Each time, she goes back to her choice and intention: What is it she wants to experience and what will be her outcome? Each time, she orients back to what she wants and what her choices are. As she reaffirms her trust in herself, she is then able to extend that trust to others.

THE COURAGE TO BELIEVE

We don't need to wear a cross around our necks, quote Scripture, carry Bibles, or try to convert others to our way of believing for the world to know we are Christians. By the way we act, speak, and interact with others we can broadcast our connection with Christ.

This clearly was the case when Peter and John came across a lame beggar at the gateway into the temple, as described in Acts 3. After the resurrection and ascension, the apostles were renewed with power, faith, and intention. They claimed their choice to be Jesus' disciples on earth and to carry out His mission as their own: to spread the good news of God's love to everyone.

When the beggar saw Peter and John, he asked them for money. After all, that's what the beggar did day after day: He asked people going into the temple to spare a little change and make an offering. Peter, however, told him they had no silver or gold to give him, but he could give the man an even greater gift. As Peter told him, "In the name of Jesus Christ of Nazareth, walk" (v. 6). Then taking the man by the hand, Peter helped him up and instantly the man's feet and ankles were strong. "He jumped to his feet and began to walk. Then he went with them into the temple courts, walking and jumping, and praising God" (v. 8).

The people in the temple were astonished. Wasn't this the lame beggar they saw outside the gate every day? Peter explained to the crowd that what had been done for the beggar was through no power or piety of his or John's, but by the grace of God through Jesus. "By faith in the name of Jesus, this man whom you see and know was made strong. It is Jesus' name and the faith that comes through him that has given this complete healing to him, as you can all see" (v. 16).

Peter and John obviously created quite a stir by their words and actions. Their choice to heal this way was risky. Their willingness to perform this miracle left them vulnerable to the same type of punishment they had just witnessed Christ endure. The testimony that they declared to the crowd brought many to believe in Jesus as the risen Savior.

When Peter and John were brought before the rulers, elders, and teachers of the law, including the high priest, they were asked,

"By what power or what name did you do this?"

Then Peter, filled with the Holy Spirit, said to them: "Rulers and elders of the people! If we are being called to account today for an act of kindness shown to a man who was lame and are being asked how he was healed, then know this… It is by the name of Jesus Christ of Nazareth, whom you crucified but whom God raised from the dead, that this man stands before you healed" (Acts 4:7–10).

Peter, a simple fisherman from Galilee, addressed the high priests directly and eloquently. Those in the temple, seeing the two men's courage and realizing that they were "unschooled, ordinary men," were astonished "and they took note that the men had been with Jesus" (Acts 4:13).

When Peter and John entered the temple that day they made a choice to heal a lame beggar who had asked them for money, but it did not end there. By their words and actions, they witnessed to Christ, which reveals their larger intention. The outcome of hundreds more people coming to believe shows what Peter and John intended all along: that everyone they met, touched, and with whom they interacted would come to know the Lord. Because of that decisive choice—to heal a lame beggar who was known to everyone at the temple—countless people came to believe.

Peter and John authored that outcome with their choices and intention, which were an extension of their faith. They, like other witnesses to Christ, changed the world because they had the courage and the conviction to act as witnesses to Jesus. Peter and John claimed the boldness of the vision of life in Christ—of a life lived abundantly. Through their intention, others too began to glimpse the possibilities of grace and truth and the promise of salvation.

Each day and in every interaction—whether with my wife or other family members, with friends, colleagues, or clients—I have choices. What I experience with them is up to me. As I learned more than twenty years ago, the outcomes reveal my intentions. If I intend to live more fully and honestly, to embrace my role as a Christian counselor while remaining open and respectful to the choices that others make, then I will experience inclusion and mutuality in my life. I will face my share of challenges and be stretched by conflicts and confrontations at times. But being a fully alive, engaged, and committed Christian demands no less of me than all I am capable of becoming.

Reflections on Choice and Intention

- With whom or in what circumstances do you find yourself feeling like a victim? Why do you think that is?

- How could you take steps to assume responsibility for creating the upsetting circumstance you find yourself in? If you were to take responsibility for authoring the upset, in what ways might you see yourself differently?

- With whom do you most consistently speak tough truths? Or who do you feel most safe in confronting and giving hard feedback to? What is it about these relationships that makes it safe for you to share honestly with them?

- Who is most honest with you? Who do you trust will give you hard feedback? What is it about your relationship that makes it safe?

Chapter 9

PURPOSE

Brothers and sisters, I do not consider myself yet to have taken hold of it. But one thing I do: Forgetting what is behind and straining toward what is ahead, I press on toward the goal to win the prize for which God has called me heavenward in Christ Jesus.
(PHILIPPIANS 3:13–14).

WHEN I WAS a young boy, I found an identity and a sense of security in athletics. By the time I transitioned from junior high to high school, however, I realized that football was not going to sustain me. The sense of community I derived from the team ended with the season. By late November or early December I was alone again, with no social connections.

In February of my sophomore year in high school, a couple of guys who were also athletes on the wrestling team invited me to come to a group with them. I was blown away. It had been two years since I had been invited anywhere. Of course I said yes; I would have agreed to anything.

169

Their invitation was to Young Life. It was a straightforward "Jesus loves you" gathering with prayers and guitar playing. From that first meeting, I felt loved and accepted. Here was the sense of belonging I had always wanted. I spent the next couple of months participating in every Young Life activity I could: retreats, workshops, Bible studies. By June, I had a profound experience that led me to make a commitment to become a lifelong follower of Christ.

My connection with Young Life was stronger than anything I had felt before. I found my purpose.

AN UNCHANGING PURPOSE

Over the years, my purpose has not changed: to experience and then to radiate and share the love of Christ. How I've lived that purpose has evolved as I've grown and matured in experience and understanding, however.

When I was in college, my vision of what it meant to be a disciple of Christ led me to devote about twenty-five hours a week directly to some type of ministry activity. After I graduated from college, and following a brief stint of working as a carpenter, I went into the ministry, serving as a college campus chaplain. Through that experience I discovered another way to live out my purpose with passion for helping people to overcome the blocks and obstacles that prevented them from taking in the love of Christ and maturing in their faith in God.

It wasn't until years later that I could see how I was trying to heal myself from the abuse I had suffered in my childhood. Because it was hidden in my unconscious at the time, I projected myself onto other people who were deeply wounded.

I tried to assist them in expanding their faith in God and experiencing a more meaningful relationship with Christ as a way of healing myself.

I began to understand how we could know in our minds that God is loving—and yet how we would have great difficulty really believing that God could possibly love us if we did not feel loved by our own parents. We cannot trust God if first we don't acknowledge how violated we have felt by the injuries—physical, emotional, psychological, or spiritual—inflicted by trusted caregivers. What we were taught and understood with our minds cannot override what we came to believe in our hearts as children.

The people I was trying to help first needed to understand how we all project onto God the collective attributes of our parents and other authority figures, the perceptions and judgments they experienced from those who had wounded them. Only as they began to learn how to resolve those hurts, could they meaningfully trust God and deepen a relationship with Him.

As I encountered people who had been deeply wounded, I realized that in order to fulfill my purpose I needed more tools and skills than just sincere concern, excellent

> We cannot trust God if first we don't acknowledge how violated we have felt by the injuries—physical, emotional, psychological, or spiritual—inflicted by trusted caregivers.

Bible teaching, and a supportive community. These realizations led me to get the professional training I needed to move from being a college chaplain to a therapist in order to help others experience the truth and grace that would salve their wounds, heal their past hurts, and lead them toward the possibility of really embracing a one-on-one, personal relationship with God.

What I didn't know at the time was how becoming a therapist would open me up to my own deep hungers and profound need to be healed. I see now that this was the necessary next step in my evolution of understanding and living out my life purpose.

The More We Experience God in Our Lives . . .

Even if you don't know what your purpose is right now, as long as you are willing to explore what it might be you will soon be on an amazing journey to know yourself and to connect more deeply with God and others. Once we embark on following a purpose we can count on God preparing us progressively and revealing to us our next steps toward living lives of meaning.

If I were to ask you what your purpose is right now, what would you say? Perhaps you've thought about this before and could answer "to radiate truth" or "to give hope and encouragement." Perhaps you think of your purpose in terms of "serving the poor" or "taking care of the less fortunate." Or you may not have any idea what your purpose is other than the pat response for so many Christians—"to love God"— although you have no idea how to carry that out. Maybe you have wrapped your purpose up with immediate goals such as pursuing an advanced degree or getting a better-paying job.

Although there may seem to be a world of difference between having a purpose to "experience my life and emotions fully" and "to own a second house in a warm climate," as a starting point it's all fine. No matter where we are, we can count on God to get us on track. The more we experience God in our lives, the more our hopes, dreams, and plans become infused with His values including grace, truth, and love. What He wants for us is to orient to something that will create movement, which ultimately brings us closer to Him.

Will had just started exploring the concept of living by his purpose. As he tried to define what that might be, he decided that, given his ample salary and his wife's family wealth, it had to be something to do with helping other people. In the meantime, he decided to give his wife, who was a real animal lover, a fortieth birthday present she would never forget.

One of her favorite animals was the black rhino, an endangered species, so he took her to Africa to see them. Toward the end of their amazing adventure Will and his wife met a man who was running a hospital—the only one around for miles. The hospital administrator, who was a Christian, told them how he had been praying for a new maternity wing on the hospital to care for mothers and babies, six out of ten of whom were born with HIV.

Instantly, Will had a vision for living out his purpose. It was right in front of him. He and his wife have since financed the building of a maternity wing on the hospital and are now seeking other ways to carry out a shared life purpose of helping others. Out of Will's desire to give his wife an amazing experience for her birthday, he came face to face with a life purpose that spoke deeply to him.

Once we each commit to a purpose, it will become the constant in our lives. Like a mast on a ship, no matter which way the wind blows our purpose can remain steadfast. It may manifest in many different ways, but purpose can guide us to how we want to experience life and share it with others, as long as we are willing to orient to it.

For many people, the discussion of purpose leads them to rediscover some basic principles about how to lead a meaningful life. This may stir up some feelings of sadness and mourning for the times when their lives were out of alignment with their purpose. Rather than shut down out of embarrassment or shame, if we remain open to our feelings we can bridge that disconnect and affirm our intention to create lives of purpose. In fact, having been off track may help us to connect authentically with others who are having similar experiences.

I have found in my workshops and working with clients that a sense of purpose often emerges from our pain—our hardship, struggle, or other adversity. For me, it was no accident that I became a therapist, having grown up in a household with an alcoholic father. To cope, I tried to do whatever I could not to upset my father and become the target of his anger and disfavor. At the same time, I took it upon myself to see to my mother's needs so that she would take care of me. It was not an ideal situation for any child, but it was through that experience that I stumbled upon one of my greatest gifts: my passion to help others.

GIVE UNTO OTHERS

One way to identify your purpose is to recognize that it is usually rooted in your own needs. What we want to do for others is really what we want and need done for ourselves. Rather than contaminating your purpose or making it selfish, your deep needs actually do the opposite. Your purpose becomes more aligned with your highest self when you are offering something to others that you know has truly benefited your life.

Seeking your purpose is not about doing what you think you should do, or what you think would be pleasing to God and others. Your purpose is what resonates within you; what gives your life meaning and engages you on many levels.

When people identify "family" as their purpose, the reasons why often reveal a hunger for connection, community, support, and belonging. Often, it goes back to their own family experience. Some people may have been narcissistically enmeshed with their parents, which led to the false assumption that their needs were being met. The other extreme is that they did not experience a sense of camaraderie, community, and family and now are trying to compensate.

Identifying family as a purpose can be used as a socially acceptable excuse to keep from engaging in one's own life. Someone can't go to a retreat or make a session because it takes time away from the family. The reality is that there will always be some family obligation. Sadly, by failing to live their lives fully and deeply, parents can rob themselves of personal growth experiences, and they miss an opportunity to be a role model for their children. When parents do not have a clear sense of their life purpose they run the risk of thinking they can vicariously fulfill their hunger for meaning through the achievement of their children. This is very confusing for both children and parents because on the surface their interest and involvement appears to be so loving.

> A sense of purpose often emerges from our pain—our hardship, struggle, or other adversity.

The normal progression is for children to grow up and launch themselves into their own lives. When the children leave, the parents experience a sense of completion and recommit themselves to each other and to deepening their relationship. It sometimes makes couples feel guilty to admit that instead of mourning an empty nest, they can now fill their lives with striving to fulfill their purpose. Instead of being the odd exception, this is actually the healthy norm. Not only does it give grown children the gift of freedom to experience their lives, but it also invigorates the parents' relationship.

Early in my personal growth work, I went away for a weekend to participate in a retreat. I knew it was costly, both in terms of time and money, and would mean that my wife would have to take care of the children by herself for the weekend. I was scared she would resent me, and I felt guilty because I did not believe I deserved to have her sacrifice for me. After returning from the retreat, I was surprised when Sue said that, based on how much she had seen me grow and change, she was fully supportive of me attending retreats in the future. Although it was a lot of extra work for her, it was worth it.

Remember, we cannot give what we do not have. The only way we can celebrate our life in Christ is to fully experience it ourselves and then to invite others into a shared experience. The good news is God will meet us wherever we are. No matter where we start, He joins us on the journey. As we grow and mature, our values will evolve and what we invest our lives in will shift. As we engage in our feelings and identify the hungers and needs below the surface, a deeper purpose will be revealed.

A Person, a Purpose, a Way of Being

Of all the people in the Bible, one of the most dramatic conversions was Paul's, as he was changed from being a persecutor of Christians to a devoted follower of Jesus. On the surface, we might say that his purpose changed just as his name did, from Saul to Paul. However, he always had a very clear purpose: honoring and serving God. What changed was his perception of who he was worshiping, along with the way he lived his purpose.

As the early Christians spread the news of the risen Christ, Saul personally engaged in a campaign against what he saw as a dangerous cult that was leading people astray. As we read in Acts 8, Saul—who had been there when the disciple Stephen was martyred—was part of a "great persecution against the church at Jerusalem. . . . Saul began to destroy the church.

177

Going from house to house, he dragged off men and women and put them in prison" (vv. 1–3).

Saul was personally threatened by the ministry of Jesus, who claimed to be the Messiah and the Son of God. What mattered most to Saul was monotheism, which set the Jewish people apart from their polytheistic neighbors. There was no way he could accept that the One God had a Son who was also fully God. Saul was also highly invested in being right. He was a Pharisee, which was the equivalent of being a Rhodes Scholar.

As we read in Acts 9, "Saul was still breathing out murderous threats against the Lord's disciples" (v. 1). For the early Christians, Saul was a zealous and dangerous man to be feared. But he was also a man of the Law; he lived by the letter of it. Silencing the Christ-followers who defied the Law as he understood it was paramount. And so he invoked the Law in order to persecute the Christians and keep them from soliciting any more followers.

> We cannot give what we do not have.

"He went to the high priest and asked him for letters to the synagogues in Damascus, so that if he found any there who belonged to the Way, whether men or women, he might take them as prisoners to Jerusalem" (vv. 1–2).

Saul's mission to Damascus, however, was interrupted. "As he neared Damascus on his journey, suddenly a light from heaven flashed around him. He fell to the ground and heard a voice say to him, 'Saul, Saul, why do you persecute me?'" (vv. 3–4).

Saul must have been shaken mightily by the voice, wondering who could be talking to him, afraid he was losing his mind. In addition, he must have been doubly troubled by the question it posed. How could he be persecuting God? All he was doing was defending God's law! This learned, eloquent man who was capable of arguing a point like a lawyer before the US Supreme Court, gave us great insight with his words. He did not ask, "What do you mean, Lord?" or "How can that be, Lord?" Nor did he defend himself, protesting, "I am not!" Instead, he posed the question that reveals the struggle in his heart against this Jesus of Nazareth, whom he tried to eradicate along with His teachings and followers: "Who are you, Lord?" (v. 5).

"I am Jesus, whom you are persecuting," he replied. "Now get up and go into the city, and you will be told what you must do" (vv. 5–6).

On the road to Damascus, Saul's world changed. In fact, when he got up from the ground and opened his eyes he could see nothing. His three days of blindness reflected Jesus' determination to get his attention and short-circuit his plan of action. The blindness was also symbolic of the fact that he was blind to God's plan and interfering with His work. Without knowing it, the one who was so convinced he was defending the truth actually could not see it.

In his conversion, the man who became known as Paul was sent by Jesus to preach the good news to the Gentiles. As he related in his testimony before King Agrippa in Acts 26, the Lord told him, "I am sending you to them to open their eyes and turn them from darkness to light, and from the power of Satan to God, so that they may receive forgiveness of sins and a place among those who are sanctified by faith in me" (vv. 17–18).

Who else but Paul could argue so convincingly about what he came to know as truth in his heart, and not just in his head? Who better to announce to people who think they know the way that they are in fact blind and cannot see the truth? It is no accident that Jesus said of Himself, "I am the way and the truth and the life" (John 14:6). The truth that Jesus spoke of was not a concept or proposition; it was a person and a way of being.

Meeting Jesus Face to Face

For any of us to follow our purpose, we must first orient to truth. For Paul, that meant opening his eyes, literally, to the truth about Jesus as the Son of God. Only then could he become retooled by God to live out his purpose in a new way.

For me, orienting to truth led me first to ministry, going to seminary, and then becoming a therapist. Along the way, my path of being a devoted follower of Christ took an unexpected direction, as I have described: doing personal growth work in a counseling practice that in many ways was anathema to my conservative Christian background. It was there, however, that I first encountered the truth about just how wounded I was. To orient to my purpose of radiating the love of God to everyone, I had to grow beyond the strictures of the world I came from so that I could see Christ in those who thought, spoke, and acted differently than me. God needed to go to some extreme measures to get my attention, just as He did with Paul.

My conversion to this truth was painful as I stretched

beyond old limits. Bob challenged me continually about being inauthentic. He told me to my face that he didn't trust me because I refused to tell the truth about when I was hurt, when I disagreed with someone, or when I was angry.

I was not used to having someone in my life who was so direct and straightforward. Historically, I had surrounded myself with people who were very careful and sensitive. They were more concerned with not hurting my feelings than in telling me the truth. I would never have stood for Bob's direct and abrupt style of communicating if I did not see the depth of his care and concern for me. Bob introduced me to the life-transforming power of truth spoken with the intent to support me in becoming my most Christlike self—though I have attempted to soften and sweeten his approach as I have since used it with others.

The Journey of a Purpose-Led Life

Committing to a purpose-led life does not mean locking into an absolute. On the contrary, it is to engage in an unfolding saga that will provide you with enough data in the short-term to keep you moving, but without any real certainty of where you are going.

Following your purpose is developmental. It connotes interaction with God and others, a process that parallels spiritual maturity. Your purpose will always lead you, flowing like a current toward a destination that you may not see. All that God asks is that we pursue our lives with abandon. It is not about being perfect or getting it right. God is concerned with us getting in the game and going all out. When we are alive and engaged, it is so much easier for God to adjust our course and redirect us as needed.

Our companion in every endeavor is Jesus, who instructed His disciples to travel light as they carried out their purpose of sharing the good news with others. Jesus told them:

"As you go, proclaim this message: 'The kingdom of heaven is near.' Heal the sick, raise the dead, cleanse those who have leprosy, drive out demons. Freely you have received, freely give. Do not get any gold or silver or copper to take with you in your belts—no bag for the journey or extra shirt or sandals or a staff; for the worker is worth his keep" (Matthew 10:7–10).

Few of us would set off on a journey with empty pockets and only the clothes on our backs. This would require an enormous amount of faith and trust in the abundance of God's resources and His powerful presence. If we did leave, we would need to continually avoid the temptation of wanting to take back control in one way or another. Our orientation would be to move in the direction of our purpose, guided by the vision we have at that moment. On our journey to pursue our life purpose, we will know we are on the path if what we are doing bears the good fruit of truth, growth, connection, relationship, and the presence of God.

Reflections on Purpose

- What inspires you to selfless sacrifice, service, compassion, and courage? What do you care most about? What would be worth dedicating your life to?

- List some of the most difficult challenges you have faced in your life: broken relationships, sickness, financial struggles? Look for common themes. Might your purpose emerge from the lessons you have learned through your experiences of hardship and suffering?

- Name where in your life you might be blind to the truth. Ask God for eyes to identify things that are presently holding you back from seeing and pursuing your mission and life purpose.

- Who do you trust to speak truth to you even though it may hurt your feelings? Consider who you may want to add to your "life team" such as those more committed to you becoming your most Christlike self rather than feeling good about and liking them.

Chapter 10

FAITH AND DOUBT

*"Unless I see the nail marks in his hands and
put my finger where the nails were, and put
my hand into his side, I will not believe"*
(JOHN 20:25).

W HEN I WAS a young Christian, mine was a simple faith. It was defined by what I experienced within the loving and accepting community of the Young Life group I joined. This was a blissful, innocent time when a tiny faith seed had been planted in my life. That phase didn't last long, however.

I wasn't satisfied with just being a new Christian. I wanted to know the Bible, to expand my mind so I would have the answers. In my first year in campus ministry, I obtained the reading list from friends who were in seminary and devoured an entire year's coursework on my own. I toted around thick books on theology, which I consumed like popcorn.

My goal was to master my understanding of Christianity, replacing any and all doubt with the Word of the one and only God, direct from the source. I trusted only the Bible and those whose expertise in interpreting the Scriptures was greater than my own. I committed Scripture to memory and learned the "right" way to interpret it. I devoted myself to apologetics to prove the validity of the Christian faith and counter any worldly doubts or arguments to the contrary. I wore my knowledge like armor.

Unwittingly, though, I became a master of dogma. I understood theology, knew the Bible inside and out, and could quote Scripture endlessly. Although I could explain doctrines and knew the creeds, it was not the same as personal faith.

My perception of God was as limited and narrow as my view of the world. I didn't dare question any of it for fear that at any moment I would find myself on the wrong side of God—just as I had worried as a child about doing anything to draw my father's anger. Questioning was neither safe nor profitable.

Even when I was in my thirties and began to surround myself with intelligent, thoughtful people who challenged my beliefs, I was terrified to look honestly at what I believed. I thought I should be through with doubting. My role was to answer others' questions, not to spend a lot of time formulating my own. If the Bible said it, I believed it and thought I was responsible to teach it. If I felt a twinge of discomfort over something in the Bible—for example, God telling Abraham to murder his son, Isaac, or the genocide of every Canaanite man, woman, and child when the Israelites invaded the Promised Land—I searched to find a biblical explanation that could satisfy me.

Cloaked in my knowledge, I hid from my feelings and from

myself. I tried to hide from God too hoping to stay under His radar, appeasing Him with good works but never drawing too much attention to myself. This behavior went against what I said I believed.

I knew from Scripture that Jesus was "the way and the truth and the life" (John 14:6). I could cite chapter and verse that proved God loved us, that every hair on our heads was numbered (Matthew 10:30). But I could never imagine a God who would be big enough and patient enough to allow me to doubt, question, and challenge Him. I was much too afraid of being punished and ostracized by the community to seriously embrace my doubts. Certainly I knew Jesus' teaching that we must become like children to enter the kingdom of heaven, but I couldn't grasp that to become childlike meant we are not expected to know all the answers. What I could not see at the time was how pride colored my perception. My desire to have all the answers was an attempt to eliminate doubt and put an end to questioning. The answers, however, wiped out the need to rely on God.

WHERE WAS LOVE?

This point was brought home to me powerfully when Bob Wright asked me if I believed that God loved me.

"Of course," I replied.

"Then why don't you live as if God loves you?" Bob challenged me. "Why don't you love yourself?"

And there it was, the truth that I had stuffed away with all my learning and understanding: that I did not live as if God loved me. The God I read about was not the God I believed in.

I lived as if God were a demanding principal of the strictest school, looking down His nose at me to see if I was an inch out of line.

Was my perception anything like the Father whom Jesus revealed? Jesus ate and drank with sinners, preached the good news of God's love and forgiveness to the common people, and challenged the know-it-alls like the Pharisees who mastered the letter of the law but lacked love in their hearts. All that I had studied and committed to memory had puffed me up into self-satisfaction that there was no question about God and the church that I could not answer.

But where was love? Did I experience God's love in my life? Was I capable of loving myself? And if I was lacking in those two areas, then how could I really love anyone else?

Confronting these questions was unsettling, to say the least, and it required a difficult and uncomfortable reckoning with my past. Facing it all, however, brought me back to a childlike state of being, open to my feelings and aware of my emotions. Finally, I could drop the façade of all that I had learned. Emptying my head of what I thought I knew, I opened my heart. And when I did, I acknowledged the questions that had nagged at me but was too afraid to acknowledge—the "why God?" and "how could this happen?"

By the time I was eighteen, however, my faith was seriously tested for the first time, when my brother Charlie and his wife had their first child, Heather.

I loved being an uncle and cherished the special role I had in Heather's life. As a toddler, however, she began to exhibit erratic behavior. Still, I loved her and spent as much time with her as I could. When Charlie and his wife had their second child it became clear that Heather's behavior had become increasingly destructive, almost violent at times. At last, she was diagnosed with an extremely rare seizure disorder, one which was degenerative. By the time she was six years old, Heather had to be institutionalized.

When I learned of this necessity, I took off for the woods, full of rage. There I poured out my heart to God. I begged Him to heal Heather so she wouldn't have to be sent away. My anger toward God for "allowing" this to happen to Heather spilled over to Charlie. How could my brother do this to his own child? I was one red-hot exposed nerve of pain and anger.

God didn't do what I'd asked. Heather's condition was as bad as ever. Now I faced a choice: I could go forward in my relationship with God or this could be the deal-breaker. Although there were no answers for why Heather had been born this way, with a condition that made her unable to live with her family, I accepted that this was something unexplained. Without knowing the answers or having the explanation, I chose to have faith. It was a major growth step, but one that I did not fully appreciate at the time.

CHILDLIKE, WITH OPEN AND QUESTIONING MINDS

Here is the paradox I have learned: True faith—deep, mature, and abiding—is full of doubt and questioning. This is not an easy truth to swallow. True believers, we tell ourselves, accept things without question. On my journey to deeper faith, however, I found the opposite to be true. Spiritual maturity is not believing only what we have been told because someone older and wiser has said it is so. Faith must be tested, wrestled, and grappled with through questioning and doubts, until it becomes one's own.

The more spiritually mature we are, the more we relinquish our need to have the answers. This gives us permission to drop our defenses and stop acting superior to others who either don't know the answers or who are in the midst of discovering what they actually do believe. Instead, we can choose to become like children. Jesus underscored the importance of being childlike in these matters when he said, "Let the little children come to me, and do not hinder them, for the kingdom of God belongs to such as these" (Mark 10:14). This does not mean we become infantile and without responsibility. Rather, we become childlike, with open and questioning minds.

> True faith—deep, mature, and abiding—is full of doubt and questioning.

Pharisees were experts in Jewish law, such as what was considered clean and unclean, or what one could or could not do on the Sabbath. Although their knowledge of the Law was vast and their self-discipline admirable, some Pharisees used these attributes like a weapon to judge and condemn others. The Pharisees seemed more interested in finding fault with someone for committing an infraction against the Law than they were in having a relationship with God—or anyone else, for that matter. Jesus had numerous run-ins with the Pharisees, who often tried to trip Him up only to fall into their own traps.

In Matthew 12:1–4 we read that Jesus was walking through some fields of grain on the Sabbath. Hungry, His disciples began to pick some heads of grain and eat them. When the Pharisees saw this, they said to Him, "Look! Your disciples are doing what is unlawful on the Sabbath" (v. 2).

You can imagine the "gotcha!" in the Pharisees' voices. This time, they must have said to themselves, they had Him. Jesus, of course, knew the Scriptures as well as any Pharisee (one could argue that he knew them even better). So when He responded, He referred to the same texts of the law that the Pharisees had used to accuse His disciples.

He answered, "Haven't you read what David did when he and his companions were hungry? He entered the house of God, and he and his companions ate consecrated bread—which was not lawful for them to do, but only for the priests. Or haven't you read in the Law that the priests on Sabbath duty in the temple desecrate the Sabbath and yet are innocent?" (vv. 3–5).

Jesus didn't mince words. In many passages, like Matthew 23:13, he directly rebuked people: "Woe to you, teachers of the law and Pharisees, you hypocrites! You shut the door of the kingdom of heaven in people's faces. You yourselves do not enter, nor will you let those enter who are trying to."

Now compare Jesus' words to the Pharisees with what He said about the little children who would inherit the kingdom of God. We see the danger of thinking we know more than we do and the wisdom of realizing we know very little. Only then can we become like children who are open to the great wonder and mystery of life all around us. Faith involves learning to be comfortable with not knowing.

There are things in life for which there are no easy answers: the epidemics that kill children in Africa or natural disasters such as the earthquake and tsunami that wiped out innocent people in Japan, for instance. Rather than searching for answers to the unknowable "why," all we have are our feelings of sadness, hurt, fear, and anger. This is what we bring to God, honestly and authentically.

In the face of the toughest questions, the only answer often is, "I don't know." This is the choice to live by faith. This attitude carries over into our lives as we keep our minds open.

For those of us who are perfectionists, instead of spending our lives trying to prepare and plan for how never to make a mistake, we need to give ourselves permission to explore and have fun learning. Learning is messy. Think of the child learning to walk who in the beginning has more falls and bumps than steps. Looking on, the parent knows the child is going to walk and soon will be running. These first steps are precious; captured on film and committed to memory. What if we viewed our lives the same way, with God as a loving parent who watches with delight, knowing that our development is dependent on our missteps and falls?

Children are very comfortable with questions; they are very aware of what they don't know. But their natural curiosity leads them to discover the world around them. When we become childlike we empty ourselves of pretenses. We admit that we don't know, that there are things we are not sure about, including what we really believe. We stop trying to sell ourselves—or anyone else, for that matter—a bill of goods based on rote memorization of catechism or Bible verses.

FATHERS OF UNBELIEF AND FAITH

Everyone has doubts. Rather than being shamed by them, what if we welcomed them instead? What if we could turn doubt on its head and see it as a blessing; an invitation to deeper, more mature, and relevant faith? The fact is the more comfortable we are with our doubts, the deeper and stronger will we grow our roots.

> In the face of the toughest questions, the only answer often is, "I don't know." This is the choice to live by faith.

As we move from young faith, based on conforming to the rules and obeying the teachings which have been handed down, into spiritual maturity and aliveness in our relationship with God, upsets and doubts will surface. Doubts are like the enzymes designed to help with our digestion—in this case, the digestion of what we believe and what we embrace as our faith.

To use another analogy, doubt is similar to building muscle through weightlifting. The muscle must be torn and broken down first in order to become stronger as it heals. Similarly, when we are courageous enough to question, our faith gets stronger, and more importantly it becomes ours—not just what someone else has passed on to us. As we mature in our faith we determine what we believe. We do this by challenging what we have been taught, deciding whether to accept or reject the tenets of our inherited faith. We must be willing to grapple with God in the process as we determine what we actually believe. God does not simply want followers. He wants thoughtful individuals who have wrestled with what they have been taught.

Consider the story in Mark 9:20–24 of the father whose son was possessed by a spirit that threw the child into convulsions. When the boy was brought to Jesus, He asked how long he had been like this. "'From childhood,' he [the boy's father] answered. 'It has often thrown him into fire or water to kill him. But if you can do anything, take pity on us and help us.'"

When we are courageous enough to question, our faith gets stronger, and more importantly it becomes ours—not just what someone else has passed on to us.

There it was: that little doubt word "if". Jesus took special note of what the boy's father said, not to make him feel worse than he already did, but to invite him to expand his faith. "'If you can?' said Jesus. 'Everything is possible for him who believes.'"

Who could blame the father, who had seen his son tormented and endangered? He had probably tried countless cures and treatments to no avail and was so desperate to help his son that he would try anything—even this "healer" named Jesus whom people were talking about. The father was willing but had been disappointed enough times to fear getting his hopes up.

Hearing Jesus' reply that "everything is possible for him who believes," the father seized the invitation to deepen his faith. Even though he wasn't there yet, he declared his intention and desire to believe, while admitting his unbelief. "Immediately the boy's father exclaimed, 'I do believe; help me overcome unbelief!'" How honest and how vulnerable this father was. Authenticity and truth are hallmarks of mature faith.

And so it is with us. When we have our doubts, we are not condemned, but rather invited to move into our uncertainty. It is a leap of faith—willingness to courageously trust and move without knowing for certain. This is true faith. Take Abraham, for example. How in the world could God have asked him to murder his son? How could a holy God ask someone to break the commandments and murder his child? Even if God were going to raise him from the dead, Abraham would still have been guilty of committing a crime against his son.

If I were Abraham I would have dismissed this prompting immediately. Instead of agreeing do something so horrific and painful, I imagine I would have used simple logic to argue against it: God would never ask someone to do something immoral and in violation of his laws and principles. Yet Abraham, the father of faith, obeyed God without knowing the answer—and he was blessed.

The Courage of a Doubting Thomas

From Jesus' death to His resurrection, the disciples went through a wide range of emotions: devastating sadness, bitter anger, paralyzing fear, and then elation. As we read in John 20, the disciples were locked away for fear that they would be arrested and killed for being Jesus' followers. Yet nothing could keep Him from connecting with them.

Jesus came and stood among them and said, "Peace be with you!" (v. 19). After He said this, He showed them His hands and His side. The disciples were overjoyed when they saw the Lord.

Then Jesus "breathed on them and said, 'Receive the Holy Spirit. If you forgive anyone's sins, their sins are forgiven; if you do not forgive them, they are not forgiven'" (v. 23).

We can imagine the excitement of the disciples seeing Jesus standing before them; it must have been incredible for everyone in that room. For the one who was not there—Thomas, called Didymus, one of the twelve chosen to follow Jesus—it was beyond belief.

When the other disciples excitedly told him, "We have seen the Lord," it was too much for Thomas. He told them, "Unless I see the nail marks in his hands and put my finger where the nails were, and put my hand into his side, I will not believe it" (v. 25).

While it's possible that he was a little jealous that Jesus would choose to appear when he was not with the others, his words reveal sadness and anger over what had happened. Jesus, whom he had followed as one of the twelve, had been arrested, tortured, and brutally executed. Clearly he struggled with his own guilt and shame for having abandoned Christ. He probably felt forsaken not only by Jesus, his friend, but also by God.

Because of his response he has earned the nickname "Doubting Thomas." However, reading the story with an awareness of our own emotions, particularly when we have felt neglected by God, we might call him "Honest Thomas." Facing what must have seemed to him to be the mass delusion of the other disciples, Thomas speaks the truth of how he feels. He cannot believe that Jesus, whom he saw dead and buried in the tomb, is alive again. The honesty of his emotions and his ability to express his doubt eventually move Thomas to profound belief.

A week later Jesus' disciples were in the house again, and Thomas was with them. Though the doors were locked, Jesus came and stood among them and said, "Peace be with you!" Then he said to Thomas, "Put your finger here; see my hands. Reach out your hand and put it into my side. Stop doubting and believe" (v. 27).

Jesus doesn't punish Thomas for expressing his doubt; rather, He pursues him. He invites him into closer relationship—putting his finger into the nail marks and placing his hand on the deep gash on His side. Jesus affirms Thomas' hunger and doubt, giving him the assurance he has sought. When his questions have been answered through what he experiences, Thomas makes a powerful statement of faith: "My Lord and my God!" (v. 28).

"Then Jesus told him, 'Because you have seen me, you have believed; blessed are those who have not seen and yet have believed'" (v. 29).

Jesus' comment is not meant to shame Thomas, but to remind the disciples what they need to do: tell others what they have seen with their own eyes and felt with their hands. They are the primary witnesses to the tragedy of the crucifixion and the miracle of the resurrection, but their faith is going to be supremely challenged after Jesus' departure, and they will need to return to this experience with Christ in order to have an unshakable faith.

Thomas becomes our proxy as we question. We who have not seen will believe because of the reliability of the witnesses. As the gospel continues, Jesus did many other miraculous signs in the presence of His disciples, which are not recorded in this book. But these are written that you may believe that Jesus is the Christ, the Son of God, and that by believing you may have life in His name (vv. 30–31).

It took courage for Thomas to express his disbelief. Most of us would have simply swallowed our doubts and conformed with the other disciples as they celebrated Christ's resurrection. If we also have his courage to be so honest, we will express our doubts, sharing our questions with God. Questions are an invitation to a mutual relationship. Questions deepen our faith. We let go of the scarcity of fear that we will be punished and exiled, and grow into a hope of God's abundance for us in a life of mature and challenging faith.

Throughout our journey we will have more questions than answers. There will be many things that we cannot prove to anyone, including ourselves. From my own experience, what I believe most deeply is not because of what I read or someone else told me. Rather, it is because of what I feel and know to be true in my soul. I have come to believe that God desires genuine dialogue with us. He is not impressed when we mindlessly repeat back what we are supposed to believe is true without question or challenge.

In my mind, God finds it refreshing when we, in the pursuit of a more authentic relationship with Christ, admit our doubt and despair. I have more doubts than answers, yet those very doubts and questions are what keep my faith fresh and alive, giving a voice to what has been unacknowledged and unspoken, leading to ever greater intimacy.

My questions have moved me into deeper connection with God, with myself, and with others. Out of my doubt, I explore in deep relationship with God. I hunger to know more and experience more. And God meets me there. He responds to each of my questions by reaching toward me to experience His presence in my life, often through my connections with others, with an ongoing invitation.

Feel.

Engage.

Risk.

Connect.

Believe.

REFLECTIONS ON FAITH AND DOUBT

- In what areas have you confused faith with certainty and the absence of doubt?

- Where do you doubt God: provision, prayer, protection? Journal about it, expressing your questions and concerns directly to Him.

- What are your next steps of faith? In what areas of your life are you willing to step courageously into the unknown?

Chapter 11

GRAPPLING TOWARD FAITH

"I have learned to be content whatever the circumstances
(PHILIPPIANS 4:11).

I SAAC AND HIS sons, Jacob and Esau, are among the most
significant characters in the Old Testament. They are note-
worthy not only because of the detail of their stories given
to us in Genesis, but also because of their direct lineage to
Abraham, the father of faith.

Despite this notable genealogy, Jacob grew up in what we
would call a highly dysfunctional family, with murderous plots,
stolen birthrights, scheming, and revenge—all the elements of
a soap opera. More importantly, we recognize that this is the
stuff of everyday life: jealousies, rivalries, family dramas, and
enmeshments. And in all of these conflicts and crises, which
we might equate with the underbelly of our human existence,
there is the opportunity to be known and redeemed by God's
loving mercy.

The story that unfolds in Genesis 25 and 27 paints a compli-
cated picture of the struggle between Jacob and Esau over

a birthright and in the midst of it their meddling mother, Rebekah. From the beginning there was great distinction between the two brothers. Esau became a skillful hunter, a man of the open country, while Jacob was a quiet man, staying among the tents. Isaac, who had a taste for wild game, loved Esau, but Rebekah loved Jacob.

The rivalry between the two brothers reached a critical point when their father was on his deathbed. Isaac called for Esau, the older son, telling him, "Prepare me the kind of tasty food I like and bring it to me to eat, so that I may give you my blessing before I die" (25:4). Overhearing this, Rebekah sent for Jacob, her favorite, and told him to take two young goats from the flock and prepare them for his father so that he would give Jacob his blessing.

Rebekah prepared the food for Isaac, while Jacob put on Esau's clothes and covered his hands and neck with goatskins to seem like his more hairy brother. The deception worked, and Isaac was fooled into giving his blessing to Jacob, thinking he was Esau. "May nations serve you and peoples bow down to you. Be lord over your brothers, and may the sons of your mother bow down to you" (v. 29). Finally, Jacob had what he sought, but at what price?

When Esau came in from hunting with the food for his father, he asked for his blessing. At that, Isaac trembled violently and demanded to know whom he had already blessed. Esau, hearing his father's words, burst out with a loud and bitter cry and said to his father, "Bless me—me too, my father!" (v. 34).

Isaac told him, "Your brother came deceitfully and took your blessing" (v. 35). Finally, Isaac gave a much different blessing to his eldest son, but it did little to make up for his lost inheritance: "Your dwelling will be away from the earth's richness, away from the dew of heaven above. You will live by the sword and you will serve your brother. But when you grow restless, you will throw his yoke from off your neck" (vv. 39–40).

Rebekah, despairing at the results of her plot, sent Jacob away until Esau's fury subsided. Jacob was on his own and headed into an uncertain future. With no choice but to accept the consequences of his actions, Jacob went to live with Laban, his mother's brother.

Laban proved to be more than his match when it came to treachery and deception, giving Jacob exactly the kind of lesson he had to learn. Having offered to work for seven years to marry Rachel, Laban's daughter, he has to work another seven years to finally get her, after being tricked into first marrying her sister, Leah.

As the families and their flocks grew, so did the conflicts; not only between Jacob and Laban, but also between Jacob and Laban's sons. In a dream, Jacob heard God's command to return to the place of his birth, the land of Canaan.

Going home, however, also meant meeting with Esau. So great was his distress over seeing his brother again, Jacob begged God, "Save me, I pray, from the hand of my brother Esau, for I am afraid he will come and attack me, and also the mothers with their children" (Genesis 30:11). Jacob came up with a plan to send his servants ahead with animals from his flocks to present to his brother, hoping to pacify him with a gift.

That night, preparing to see the brother who had sworn to kill him, Jacob had a wrestling match that he would never forget: a man so strong he hobbled Jacob by dislocating his hip. Finally the man told Jacob to let him go, for it was daybreak. But Jacob told him he would not let go until the man blessed him. The man asked him his name. He replied, "Jacob."

Then the man said, "Your name will no longer be Jacob, but Israel, because you have struggled with God and with men and have overcome" (v. 28). After the man blessed him, Jacob called the place Peniel, which means "Face of God," saying, "It is because I saw God face to face, and yet my life was spared" (v. 30).

Finally the moment arrived: Jacob and Esau reunited after more than twenty years.

Jacob looked up and there was Esau, coming with his four hundred men; so he divided the children among Leah, Rachel, and the two maidservants. He put the maidservants and their children in front, Leah and her children next, and Rachel and [her son] Joseph in the rear. He himself went on ahead and bowed down to the ground seven times as he approached his brother.

Esau ran to meet and embrace Jacob. A lot of painful learning and growing had happened in the years these brothers were apart. Esau had mellowed over the years and forgave his brother for his scheming. Jacob had learned humility after tasting his own medicine when it came to deceptiveness in his dealings with Laban. Because he was willing to grapple with God, Jacob—renamed Israel—became a better man in the process and was able to re-enter into relationship with his brother, Esau.

LIVING IN FAITH, TRUTH, AND CONNECTION

Having relied on my own strength and ability to defend myself for so much of my life, it seemed I needed to be incapacitated by a degenerative condition in my hip to learn that my real strength came from God and my relationships.

I am not saying that God caused the osteoarthritis. However, God was with me every moment, and I believe He used my physical condition and my need for surgery to deepen my connection with Him. It's no surprise, then, that as I opened up to a more real and intense experience of God, wrestling with Him as Jacob did, my relationships with my family also deepened. I learned to stop relying on my self-sufficiency and start allowing Sue and others to take care of me. As I recuperated, I grew to love the many things my family did for me, from helping me put on my socks to driving me around.

That is what our life of faith does: We let go of everything in order to receive God's abundance. We are broken down to be built up again. It happens in countless ways, big and small. If we can accept where we are, never are we in need. God is always with us—engaging, grappling, wrestling. The journey is never complete as long as we are alive.

Becoming more Christlike stretches us in uncomfortable places, beyond our boundaries and over the thresholds of our old limits. We can no longer afford to be shut down in any part of our lives. A deep disappointment, bitter loss, or devastating hardship forces us to ask the deeper questions. We cannot numb ourselves to the pain; instead, the sharpness of the emotion becomes a knife that cuts through to the core issue—Where is God in this? If we shy away from this question, the unexpressed doubts eat away inside, undermining our ability to heal, to reconnect, to experience hope and healing. To be like Christ is to be alive in all of it: in the joy, the pain, and the sorrow.

Often we mistakenly believe God is our worst critic and the ultimate source of our guilt and shame. We fail to remember, however, that the true sources of our painfully mistaken beliefs are ourselves, our parents, and family members.

> Becoming more Christlike stretches us in uncomfortable places, beyond our boundaries and over the thresholds of our old limits.

Through our own growth and development, we understand and accept that the yearning we share with all of humanity is to be loved and accepted unconditionally. This is what many see as grace. The foundation of all of our attempts to effectively learn, grow, and develop is our confidence in the truth and our commitment to grace. As we learn to have grace for ourselves, we gradually come to believe that God loves each of us unconditionally. It is in an environment of grace that we can safely risk discovering and being our most authentic selves. The Funnel of Truth I described in Chapter 3 can help us do that by uncovering our deepest truths. These are the truths that shape our yearnings and our most deeply held beliefs about ourselves, others, and the world. As we mature, we learn that truth is often a matter of faith.

Seeking to become more spiritually mature, we recognize

the importance of our feelings and how they contain the truth of our experience. We learn to identify our feelings because feelings reflect the truth of our hearts. When we hide our fear, hurt, sadness, anger, unworthiness, rejection, abuse, and abandonment, we keep ourselves from connecting fully with others—and with God.

No longer satisfied to live in our heads in a world we think we can control, we risk feeling and expressing what's in our hearts. Feeling more deeply our fear, hurt, sadness, and anger, we become more honest with ourselves and others, including God. Admitting our fears empowers us to develop the confidence to be open and vulnerable. Acknowledging our sadness and hurt, we affirm our hunger to connect with others. Learning to access our anger and express it responsibly, we assert ourselves in relationships without damaging our connections with others. We are on the path to creating meaningful intimacy with ourselves as well as with one another.

> Admitting our fears empowers us to develop the confidence to be open and vulnerable.

With grace and truth, we accept ourselves and each other just as we are. With purpose and intention, we embrace our responsibility to choose how we are going to live and who we are going to be. We commit to using our abilities and talents to love and support one another.

THE MORE WE GRAPPLE, THE MORE GOD ENGAGES

Here is the vision I hold: to engage more fully in life than I ever thought possible; to be open and expressive with my feelings; to tell the truth in the moment; to be more connected within myself and in my relationships with others and with God.

Living a journey of faith has taken me far beyond what I thought was possible into an unknown dimension within my own life. What allows us to engage in the game is grace: the unconditional and unimaginable love and acceptance of God. That is all we need for this journey, for we are never alone.

We might wonder how and where this happens, perhaps expecting the "bolt of lightning" of Paul's conversion or the rapturous transformation of the transfiguration. Our journey of faith, however, leads us to seek an experience of transcendence in everyday life. Granted, it may seem that the worries, busyness, obligations, troubles, and the responsibilities that come with living each day would get in the way of feeling oneness with Almighty God. However, it is exactly in these very ordinary things that we can encounter the most extraordinary of all: Jesus within us and among us, as real to us as He was to His disciples.

The words of the Lord's Prayer speaking of "our daily bread" do not address needs that were somehow special or more worthy of God's time and attention. Instead, Jesus invites us to meet God in the most basic of our needs, our daily bread— whatever it is we need each day to nourish us body, mind, and spirit. He is ultimately the source of all nourishment— not simply through prayer, meditation, and reading of the Bible. God may meet our needs through the kind word of a stranger, a blue sky, a bird in flight, a passage from a book—through anything and in any way. God is present when we are conscious and seeking Him.

There are times when an out-of-the-ordinary incident takes us deeper. It may be a joyful event, such as the birth of a child or grandchild that brings us to a higher level of consciousness of God in our lives. Our emotions are so powerful and accessible, we feel ourselves being cracked open like eggshells to reveal the soft, vulnerable parts inside, and we are forever changed. Perhaps the catalyst is a deeply difficult circumstance such as a health issue, your own or a loved one's; or problems such as divorce, overcoming addiction, death, loss of a job or financial security, or another challenge.

Whatever has rocked our world shakes us to the core, and we are no longer sure who we are in that moment without whatever it is that we've come to rely on, whether physically, emotionally, psychologically, or spiritually. We are on the floor (perhaps literally), grappling with an unknown adversary. Twisting and turning, we are pinned down time and again, but we do not give up the struggle. We persevere, testing ourselves and stretching the limits of our capacity to feel.

Relationships are not always easy, and often we need to develop and strengthen our skills. On this journey, you will need grace and truth, to be able to look at yourself, your life, and your relationships. Feeling your feelings means encountering and admitting your hurt, fear, sadness, and anger, which can be uncomfortable for many of us. You will never go through it alone, though. At every step, from the depths of sadness to indescribable joy, you will be accompanied by Jesus, your Savior, your brother, your friend, who longs to know you and have you know Him.

With each step you must decide that you are loved, that the God who made you loves everything about you. You must learn to live from the assumption that there is nothing shameful, unlovable, or lacking about you. God is crazy about you, and wants you to get to know Him—and yourself—better.

Reflections on Grappling toward Faith

- In the story of Jacob, in what ways are you like Esau? How are you like Jacob?

- Are you aware of areas in your life where you are afraid to be honest with God? If so, risk telling the truth about what you have been withholding. Practice stepping out in faith and start engaging with Him.

- Has there been a time when you did "go to the mat" with God? What was it about, and how did your grappling with Him impact your relationship?

- How would you like to see your relationship with God deepen and mature?

Center for
Christian Life Enrichment

At the Center for Christian Life Enrichment, our mission is to see you live life abundantly. We believe personal transformation is both a science and a matter of faith. We break down the process of growing and changing into understandable and practical steps. We build upon the core values and principles of authentic Christianity and draw from existential, developmental, Adlerian, and humanistic schools of psychology and integrate the best of those theories and methodologies.

We know that individuals often transform with the help of others. We emphasize the priority of relationships and utilize one-on-one counseling along with small groups. We have a wide variety of small groups and have found that individual therapy along with groups is the most potent and transformative combination.

Rich Blue leads and supervises an outstanding staff of dedicated therapists and Christ followers. Our staff team has a wide range of specialties and we are able to serve the needs of most of the people who reach out to us. In cases where we do not have a particular expertise, we are able to refer individuals to other trained professionals to ensure that each person receives the care they need.

LIVE LIFE ABUNDANTLY

To learn more about our services
contact us at info@cle.us.com
or call the office at 847-272-3684 ext. 100.

2ND ORDER MINISTRIES
A journey of divine discovery

2nd Order Ministries is a not-for-profit foundation dedicated to teaching, training and equipping pastors and parishioners to promote the love of God and develop dedicated disciples of Christ.

2nd Order Ministries strives to be agents of personal and spiritual transformation through integrating the most potent and efficacious theories and methodologies of human development with the principles and practices of authentic Christianity.

If you would like to find out more about the work and ministry we do, and partner with us in any way, please contact us at: **www.2ndorderministries.com**

CONTINUE THE CONVERSATION

If you believe in the message of this book and would like to share in the ministry of getting this important message out, please consider taking part by:

- Writing about *Surprised by God* on your blog, Twitter, Instagram and Facebook page.

- Suggesting *Surprised by God* to friends and send them to the book's website www.surprisedbygod.com

- When you're in a bookstore, ask them if they carry the book. The book is available through all major distributors, so any bookstore that does not have it in stock can easily order it.

- Encourage your book club to read *Surprised by God.*

- Writing a positive review on www.amazon.com

- Invite Rich Blue to speak at an event by visiting www.surprisedbygod.com.

- Purchasing additional copies to give away as gifts.